FROM QUEENSLAND TO
THE GREAT BARRIER REEF

From Queensland to the Great Barrier Reef

A Naturalist's Adventures in Australia

by

NOEL MONKMAN

F. R. M. S.

Doubleday & Company, Inc.

Garden City, New York

1958

Library of Congress Catalog card number: 58–5949

First published in the United States of America, 1958

To

MY WIFE, KITTY

The constant companion and fellow-worker, who forsook her profession, the music she loved so well, to come a-wandering in the wilds with me.

FOREWORD

I HATED school. Even today, the hectoring clamour of a school bell gives me a feeling of nausea, and my leg muscles quiver as if urging me to make for the safety of the nearest bushland. I was an incorrigible truant, and considered the only answer to punishment for truancy was immediately to play the wag again.

Now, as I look back to those distant days, I realize I was trying to secure good attendance marks at the only schools I loved—the bush, the rivers, lakes, ponds, and the pools of the sea-shore at low tide. Here lived my friends, all the furred, feathered, scaled or many-legged folk, and the busy people who were invisible until I peeped at them through the magic window of my microscope.

From the age of nine years I had three absorbing hobbies—the microscope, photography, and music. My mother was a professional concert singer and pianist, so perhaps my years of later life, also as a musician, a 'cellist, were preordained; but my love of the wild places and their peoples, and my camera and microscope, remained undiminished.

Eventually the theatre became as cramped as a schoolroom, so again I played the wag. The truant inspector has never caught up with me. Once more I roam happily in the wilds with my cameras and microscopes. I have a companion now, my wife, Kitty, another musician, who has played the wag with me for many years.

NOEL MONKMAN

Dangar Island,
Hawkesbury River,
New South Wales.

CONTENTS

ILLUSTRATIONS

FROM QUEENSLAND TO
THE GREAT BARRIER REEF

CHAPTER I

SNARING SAURIANS

THE river lay still—not a ripple corrugated its placid surface. The tropic sun glared down; the shafts of sunlight filtering through the leaves of the mangrove-lined banks were like shining spears pinning the tortuous roots of the mangroves to the oozing, slimy mud. Those misshapen roots, twisted and intertwined, crept above the surface of the mud as if even the trees were loath to plunge their roots beneath that fetid surface. Not a breath of wind stirred the leaves, but the scene was not silent. A ceaseless, irritating hum dinned at the ear-drums. Mosquitoes were there in countless billions, and sandflies which, although they made no sound, could drive man or beast almost insane with their ravenous appetites.

Yet the beauty of the river was compensation for all else. Thickly dotted over its surface, like gorgeous lotus flowers in an Eastern lake, rested blossoms fallen from the jungle trees miles upstream. Imperceptibly the blossoms moved—gradually this movement increased, it could hardly be said they moved faster, but surely they were moving less slowly; the pull of the sea in this tidal river was becoming apparent. Slowly the tempo increased, and round the bend of the river a new carpet of blossoms came gliding into view.

In their midst drifted a boat, completely hidden in a canopy of leaves. Two men lay in the boat concealed amidst the leafy branches that were lashed to the gunwales. Quiet and still they lay, but their eyes and ears were alert. Were they watching for the sight of hostile natives with bows and poisoned arrows, or were they listening for the monotonous rhythm of native drums awaking jungles natives to the knowledge that white men had invaded their territory? Not so; this was not some river of the Belgian Congo, or a waterway of head-hunting Dyaks: this was a river in the far north of Australia, and although high-powered rifles lay beside my companion and me, we had no wish to use them, they were there for emergency only; any shooting I wished to do would be done with the camera.

I

On this expedition we searched for the huge man-eating crocodiles that inhabit these tropical tidal rivers. I sought no dead specimens, but wished to secure them alive for a zoo, and to make a motion-picture record of the trapping of the monsters.

Australia possesses two distinct species of crocodiles, *Crocodilus porosus*, the great salt-water crocodile, and *C. johnstoni*, a smaller crocodile, peculiar to Australia, which prefers fresh water and is not found in the salt-water rivers. In the winter months, drifting silently down-river towards the sea, one may get within camera range of the big salt-water crocodiles sunbathing on the mudbanks.

These tropical tidal rivers are a never-ending attraction for naturalists, for wild life is usually abundant. The dense jungle cascades down the mountain-sides into the river, and the trees, festooned with wild orchids, are burdened with nesting birds. The interlaced rope-like lianas, those strangling, botanical thugs of the jungle, make innumerable bridgeways for the snakes that glide from tree to tree on their silent but deadly business, while strange and colourful insects flit or creep through the shadowy depths of the forests. Even the mudbanks where the crocodiles bask have a teeming population. One of these mud-dwellers is an extraordinary creature, a fish that gazed at us with watchful, goggling eyes from the low branch of a tree, then dropped from the tree, walked across the mud, and dived out of sight into a small puddle. It was *Periophthalmus*, the walking fish, which would drown if held under water for too long—a reminder of the path of evolution, and our own dimly seen ancestors who left the ancient seas to breathe air, to climb the trees, and who eventually became men.

As we drifted slowly downstream the air became heavy with a nauseating stench that increased as we rounded a bend in the river. For more than half a mile the trees along one bank were festooned with thousands of flying-foxes. These queer blossom- and fruit-eating bats are so fond of each other's odorous company that, after their individual foraging for food during the night, they return before dawn to make a community camp in the trees where they sleep throughout the day. In these camps they cling to the branches, hanging head downward, and look like clusters of dark, withered leaves. So densely do they congregate on the branches that occasionally a weak limb breaks, and down comes the branch, foxes and all. If this limb is fairly low on the tree the foxes on it have no time to become air-borne before they crash, and as they fall to the ground there is a pandemonium of shrill screeches that is taken up by the whole colony. The flying-fox is unable to fly straight off the ground, and so these crest-fallen members of the colony shuffle along to the trunks of the trees up which they climb with extraordinary agility, using the grappling hooks on their wings to swing themselves aloft. Here they squabble and push until they have made room for themselves on an already packed branch, whereupon they fold their wings around their bodies and once more hang like a bunch of withered foliage.

As we drifted past this camp we got our first sight of a crocodile. A branch, heavily laden with flying-foxes, suddenly snapped, and unable to regain their balance they fell with futile flappings of their membranous wings towards the surface of the water. There was a sudden swirl in the water beneath them, and a great ugly head appeared above the surface. Right into the gaping jaws of a crocodile plunged the unfortunate flying-foxes. The terrible jaws closed with a thudding snap, and then there was only a broken branch drifting out of a widening circle of ripples.

This was a suitable place to put in a crocodile trap, but if you have ever smelt flying-foxes, you will understand our reluctance to linger in the vicinity. It is a revolting stench, and we decided to let the crocodile enjoy his highly seasoned meal in peace, and drifted downstream for a breath of fresh air.

The screeching din of the flying-foxes had become merely a faint chanter to the bagpipe drone of the mosquitoes when we saw in the shadow of the mangroves the tracks of a crocodile on a shelving mud-bank. Starting the engine, we swung the boat into the bank. As we stepped out of the launch we sank to our knees in the oozing mud, and before we could take a second step the mosquitoes had found us. Unless one has actually experienced their attentions in tropical man-grove country, one can have no conception of the quantity and quality of their ferocious attacks. As we made our way painfully through the mud towards the crocodile tracks, I could see mosquitoes descending in hordes on my companion, and by the time we reached the tracks he looked as though he was swathed in a dark grey felt, so thickly

3

were mosquitoes clustered upon him. I knew that I must look the same, for already I could feel the bloodthirsty insects at work. In irritation I ran my hand down my arm to brush them off, with the result that my arm looked as if it had been smeared with raspberry jam, the "jam" being my own blood mixed with the crushed bodies of the mosquitoes. I remembered seeing an aboriginal under similar circumstances plastering himself with mud, so we gathered handfuls of the slimy muck and plastered it over the more exposed parts of our bodies. It certainly helped to ward off the hungry pests until it cracked away as the mud dried.

From the size of the tracks on the bank this must have been a big crocodile, for a broad furrow was gouged out of the mud as if the trunk of a large tree had been dragged out of the water. On each side of this groove made by the body of the crocodile were the tracks of great webbed feet, with the marks of the terrible claws biting deep into the earth. These saurians, like their ancient ancestors, grow to a great size. There are records of *Crocodilus porosus* nearly thirty feet in length, and I have seen several of over twenty feet.

During the winter months a crocodile will select a mudbank to which it will return every day, drag its ponderous bulk out of the water, and lie basking in the sun. Such a spot is ideal for setting a trap, so, taking axes, we cut a quantity of stout mangrove saplings and drove them into the mud to build a fence leading from the river up the bank to the spot selected for the trap. Crocodiles are extremely wary, and will, if possible, circle round and reconnoitre a bait before seizing it. The fence guides them towards the trap in the direction one wishes them to enter. If they get at the bait from the back of the trap, they can take it without being caught.

The trap is simple yet ingenious in principle, not unlike a gigantic mouse-trap, but it differs in being designed not to kill, but only to capture. A big tree with stout branches is chosen, and a heavy pulley block is firmly wired to a limb projecting over the river bank. Through this pulley is passed a stout wire hawser. One end of the hawser is fastened to a heavy log, the other end has a running noose. The log is then hauled aloft until it reaches the pulley, where it is kept in position by a simple trigger arrangement with a cord running from it to the bait. The running noose on the hawser is now put into

4

Freshwater crocodiles sunning themselves around a pool.
(From the film *Catching Crocodiles*.)

"he fish gazed at us from
 low branch of a tree."
om the film *Nature's
le Jokes.*)

There is something essentially prehistoric about the crocodile.
(From the film *Catching Crocodiles*.)

Crocodile trap showing noose.

position. The place chosen for this loop depends upon the size of the tracks that have been seen on the banks, the idea being that the crocodile should go a certain distance through the loop before it can reach the bait. From a study of the tracks one can estimate fairly accurately what the distance would be from the tip of the snout to a point behind the front legs. When a crocodile passes through this loop it seizes the bait and commences to drag it away. The pull on the bait sets the trigger off in the tree above, and the heavy log attached to the other end of the loop falls, causing the noose to close tight about the crocodile's middle. The weight of the log continuously prevents the loop from working loose, no matter how furiously the captive may struggle.

Many trappers use live dogs or goats as bait, considering that the cries of the unfortunate creatures will attract the crocodiles to the trap. To me this has always seemed inhuman, and I have found that dead goat—very dead goat—is equally effective. We carried several bags of dead goat aboard the launch, and as it ripened in the tropic sun it became most obnoxious to human nostrils, but most appealing to a crocodile which prefers its food "high". The stench was unbearable, so we sent the bait higher still by tying it to a rope, then hauling it to the masthead.

The crocodile that had left its tracks in the mud where the trap was now placed was almost certainly somewhere in the vicinity, but if we remained anywhere near the trap the man scent would warn it of danger, and it would be unlikely to go near the trap. So we went aboard the launch to continue our search for further likely places to set more traps.

It was no longer possible to drift, for the river appeared to be defying the laws of gravitation and was flowing upstream, so we started the engine and continued on our way down-river. As we proceeded, the strong scent of the sea became noticeable, and the sweet brackish taste of the river water told us that the tide was once more sweeping inwards. In navigating uncharted rivers it is as well to keep in mind that deep water is generally alongside the bank where the hills sweep right to the water's edge, and shallow water on the flat country side.

As the boat rounded a bend in the river, I saw a queer sight. Yards out from the steep bank the green top of a palm projected above the water. I was puzzled, for the palm looked as if it were alive and growing, but it was obviously impossible for a palm to take root under a river. I steered the boat between the bank and the palm. There was a terrific crash which threw me to the deck. My companion, who had been at the engine, yelled out that water was coming in at the bows. Making a grab for the tiller, I swung the boat around and beached her on a shelving mudbank. Some damage had been done and water was squirting through seams that had sprung in the bows. We got to work on the repairs and finished the job of caulking the seams with torn-up singlets soaked in engine gasket cement. This proved effective, and after pumping out we were once more seaworthy.

It was not until a day or two later, when we returned up-river at low tide, that I discovered the cause of the accident. At some time a landslide or cyclone had caused a palm to fall outwards into the river, but the roots had kept a firm grip of the earth, and the palm had continued growing although the trunk was no longer vertical, but grew out horizontally from the bank towards the middle of the river, in the same position as a pipe held in a man's mouth. The feathery top of the palm had grown upwards towards the air and sunshine, and now was turned up like the bowl of the pipe. The horizontal trunk, submerged at high tide, was quite invisible in the muddy water, and I had driven the boat head on to it.

By the time we had finished working on the boat it was coming on dusk, and the mosquitoes were emerging in clouds from the surrounding jungle. Their ceaseless blood-sucking was annoying enough, but their monotonous droning hum was almost as irritating; so we decided that instead of putting up mosquito nets on the deck we should continue down-river and anchor at sea, where a cool breeze should enable us to sleep without the net. Many a time on tropical rivers I have gone to sleep on the deck of a boat beneath a mosquito net, to wake with a feeling that a wild animal was gnawing at my arm: the breeze had blown the net against me, and, where it touched, the mosquitoes were obtaining a good meal through the meshes of the net. On one such occasion I woke to almost total darkness although sleeping in the open on a night of full moon. A sharp shake of the net caused a blanket of mosquitoes to lift from it, and I caught a glimpse

"With jaws agape, the crocodile regarded me with a cynical smile."

The snouts of the crocodiles were worked through the meshes and ed. (From the film atching Crocodiles.)

The palm that caused the accident. At high tide the trunk was under water.

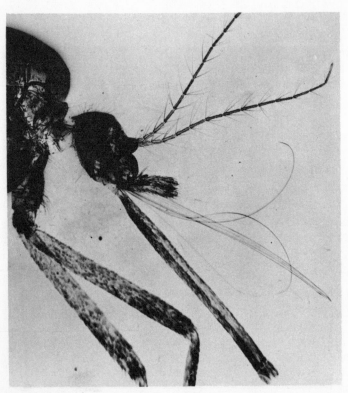

It is the female mosquito that seeks our blood. The sharp scalpel pierces the skin, and the blood is sucked up through the tubular tongue. (Greatly magnified.)

of the river with a full tropic moon gleaming down upon it before the mosquitoes once again settled on the net and almost blotted the scene from view. It may seem that I am putting an undue emphasis on the prevalence of mosquitoes, but it has been my experience that whenever I searched for crocodiles, the mosquitoes have searched for me; and although I have not always been successful in *my* hunting they have never failed to discover their quarry. Still, perhaps I should not feel too hardly about them, for they indirectly saved my life.

The accident to the boat had made us late in reaching the sea and night had descended by the time we reached the river mouth. The moon had not yet risen as we blithely continued on to what we thought was deep water. There was a sinister whispering sound from under the boat and it slowed up slightly. Hurriedly I swung the tiller over, for that sound could only mean shoal waters and we were almost aground. Again the boat picked up speed and we went merrily ahead for a few yards. Again I heard a sound like soft fingers stroking the hull, and swung the tiller in the opposite direction. It was clear going for a couple of seconds, and then, with a harsh grating noise, the boat came to a dead stop. We were well and truly aground on the bar at the river mouth. Pulling off shirt and trousers, we jumped overboard and commenced heaving and shoving to get the boat free. The bow slid off the bank and she was afloat again, but not for long—she moved only a few feet back and the stern was aground. Our only hope was to reconnoitre and find if a channel of deeper water led out from the mudbank. By this time the mosquitoes had found us again, so I climbed aboard and put my shirt on, thinking that at least it might keep me from being bitten on my back and shoulders while we waded round seeking for deep water. I jumped back into the water and had hardly arrived there when there was a sudden splash and swirl in the darkness—the sound of snapping jaws—and I was jerked off my feet and dragged under water. A crocodile had evidently mistaken my shirt, which was billowing round me, for part of me. There were a few seconds of frantic scrambling and whirling under water and I felt my back pressed down on the mud for a moment or two. Then came a vicious jerk—my shirt was ripped from my body—and I was free!

I have no recollection of even touching the side of the boat, but like the man on the flying trapeze I sailed through the air with the

7

greatest of ease, and landed asprawl on the deck. I had no sooner arrived there than my companion arrived alongside me in the same bird-like manner, but he had not got off so lightly. The crocodile, evidently bewildered with my shirt wrapped round its head, had swung away from the boat, but in passing had scraped its rough, scaly body along my friend's leg, tearing the skin like a gravel rash. That was enough. We decided to stay on deck under our mosquito nets and wait for the morning tide to lift us off the bar.

As I lay there in the darkness, I had a guilty feeling that perhaps I wasn't being quite fair. I should perhaps, in gratitude, dispense with the net and let the mosquitoes feed unhindered. After all, they were responsible for my still being in the land of the living.

CHAPTER 2

THE TRAP IS SPRUNG

W HEN we awoke next morning a thin column of smoke was rising through the jungle roof about a mile along the shore from the river mouth. It was too narrow a column to be a jungle fire, and in this part of the world we considered it would almost certainly be rising from a native camp.

The morning tide had lifted the boat, setting us free from the mud, so we gingerly made our way into deep water and sailed along the coast towards the smoke column. Our surmise proved correct; we had gone only a little way along the coast when we saw some native boys wading in the shallows spearing fish. Dropping anchor, we rowed ashore and went with the boys to their camp.

On this expedition I was anxious to secure a motion-picture record of the nesting habits of the crocodiles, so at the camp I enlisted the aid of two of the natives, promising them ten sticks of trade tobacco for each crocodile nest they found. This sounded real wealth to the boys, and I was delighted to have such experienced bushmen on the job.

We arranged to meet the two natives up the river; they were to leave from the encampment and search for crocodile nests along the bank of the river until they reached the boat. We took the boat upstream again to this meeting-place, anchored there, then went ashore to search for nests on the river bank upstream from the anchorage. That night we arrived back at the boat weary, soaked with sweat, and dishevelled and torn from forcing our way through the dense jungle. But our efforts had been unrewarded, for not a nest had we found. I was hopeful that the native boys, with their uncanny bushcraft, had been more fortunate. We found them contentedly asleep, but with no crocodile eggs in their dilly-bags. Another day gone—and no film in the box. What a life!

In the morning I questioned the natives regarding the territory they had combed, so that we would not uselessly overlap in our search;

but I sensed a hesitancy in their replies which made me suspicious.

"You fella boys come walkabout longa me," I said.

"We white fellas go walkabout longa way you bin walkabout."

The look of consternation on their faces was significant; something needed investigating. Despite the boys' very evident reluctance, I insisted that they accompany us as we started off downstream going over their tracks of the previous day. We had not proceeded more than a few hundred yards when we found the explanation of the boys' unwillingness to accompany us. They had found a crocodile nest only a short distance from the anchorage, and the eggshells, emptied of their contents, told their own story. The natives considered crocodile eggs a most piquant dish, and not even the promise of many sticks of tobacco had prevented them from enjoying a hearty meal. I could not help laughing, for the boys now looked as miserable as if they had swallowed the winning ticket in the lottery. Seeing that I was prepared to treat the matter as a joke, one of the natives chuckled, then said, "Boss come walkabout—findum nest longa grass."

We followed him down-river for about a mile, then to my astonishment he turned at right angles to the river and continued away from the water for quite a distance. I felt sure we were to be disappointed, for I thought crocodiles would make their nests just a few feet above the level of the river. However, I followed on without comment. About five or six hundred feet back from the river we broke into a grassy clearing, and there, undisturbed in the centre of it, was a fine big crocodile nest. I think the explanation of its distance from the river must lie in the floods, and king tides that are common in these tidal rivers. At such times the waters would cover the banks for a considerable distance in to the flat country near the river mouth. The instinct of the crocodile evidently causes it to make its nest where it will be beyond the reach of flood waters.

The native had led us straight to the nest, so it was obvious that he had found it the previous day, but had not reported it, hoping that the price of crocodile eggs would rise. It did not need a glance at the wrinkles on his dusky face to know that he was not born yesterday. However, my laughter over the first nest had evidently pleased him and he had decided to be generous. He was a good judge of human nature and did not lose by having made a meal of the eggs from the first nest, for in my delight at his discovery of this second nest, I paid out an absurd price in tobacco.

For many yards round the nest the grass and dead leaves had been raked up into a mound about three feet high in the centre and with a circumference of about thirty feet. Carefully I dug down into the mound, and about two feet from the top were more than forty eggs. They lay close together in a rough circle in the midst of the rotting leaves and grass. The warmth of the nest was astonishing; it was not only the warmth of the tropic sun, for the farther one dug down, the warmer it became. The rotting vegetation was undoubtedly generating a surprising amount of heat. This relieves Mrs Crocodile of the necessity of sitting on her eggs and incubating them. It is just as well that this is so, for she would undoubtedly break them, the shells being comparatively fragile and, surprisingly, not so much larger than a duck egg, but without the pointed end of a bird's egg. The limy shell is similar to that of a hen's egg, but thin and easily cracked. Beneath this is a very tough, parchment-like skin. It was evident that superficial cracking of the outer, limy shell need not necessarily cause the destruction of the developing embryo, for I opened several eggs that had the outer shell slightly cracked, and found tiny crocodiles not ready to emerge. Although prematurely born and unable to survive for long, they displayed the characteristics of their species by snapping viciously at the hand that liberated them. They made good specimens for the formalin jar.

The utter savagery of *Crocodilus porosus* is hard to believe unless witnessed. Not one nice thing can be said in their favour. From the minute they are born until they die they live in a state of smouldering rage, ready to snap into action at any moment.

Throughout tropical Australia one finds place-names such as Alligator River, Alligator Creek, Alligator Swamp, or Alligator Lagoon, and crocodiles are almost invariably referred to by the inhabitants of these parts as alligators. This is incorrect; there are no alligators native to Australia, only the two species of crocodiles, *C. porosus,* and *C. johnstoni.* The difference between the crocodile and the alligator lies not only in a differently shaped snout—the alligator's is shovel-shaped, the crocodile's is spatulate—but in a different formation of the jaws. The lower jaw of the crocodile has canine teeth which fit into a notch in the upper jaw so that the teeth are always partly visible. This is not so with the alligator. There are also further differences in the feet.

But the greatest difference lies in the savagery and strength of the two creatures. The alligator is quite a sleepy and good-natured beast compared to the crocodile, and does not possess the remarkable speed and agility of the latter. A proof of this was given when a Florida alligator fourteen feet in length was being transported to the New York zoo. A small ten-foot Australian crocodile was put in the same cage. Next morning the alligator was found dead with terrible wounds on its body, but the crocodile was quite uninjured, and had dispatched its much larger cousin with the greatest of ease.

Near the anchorage I had seen tracks of several more crocodiles, so set the natives to work cutting saplings, while my companion and I built and baited several traps. It was certainly a relief to get rid of the smelly bait. The odour was so all-pervading that every meal we ate tasted of long-dead goat. One set of tracks, on a bank where we built a trap, amazed me by their huge size. I was not fortunate enough to secure the crocodile that had made these tracks; it was evidently too wary to enter the trap, but it must have been a monster. I estimated it as close to thirty feet.

There is something essentially prehistoric about the crocodile. It would seem to be a relic of the days of the terrible reptiles when the dinosaurs fought bloody battles in the steamy swamps of the ancient world. Yet strangely enough, the crocodile cannot be traced back to the Age of Reptiles, although fossils have been found in Europe of alligators that lived as far back as the Pliocene period of the Cainozoic era. This is not such a distant period in the history of our world, since Cainozoic means recent life, and it was in this era that evolution developed man and many other animals closely related to those found on earth today. The dinosaurs lived in the Mesozoic Age, which is many millions of years earlier. So man and the crocodile would seem to have evolved almost side by side. This would seem a suitable place to mention that those stories or sketches depicting a skin-clad and club-armed caveman riding on, or being chased by, a dinosaur are amusing fairy tales, for primitive man and the dinosaur were not contemporaries by many millions of years. However, the crocodiles are very distant cousins of the dinosaurs, and evolution was trying out in the dinosaurs many of the anotomical details of future crocodile structure. For instance, while the Dinosauria were finding out how the transverse processes and ribs of crocodilian character would stand up to hard usage, the teeth of the crocodile were being given a trial by a marine monster called the Plesiosaurus, which had teeth like a crocodile, whale-like paddles, ribs like a chameleon, and a long, serpent-like neck. But even though the dinosaur and the crocodile did not share the same river or swamp in those faraway days, the crocodile of today has so many characteristics of its ancient, awe-inspiring ancestors that it gives us quite a good glimpse of life as it was in the dim yesterdays before man was—man.

That night, as we lay under our nets, the breeze blowing down-river brought to our ears a sound of bellowing like bulls in a branding yard. It could have been the mating call of a male crocodile, but in the morning I thought it well to examine our first trap upstream. Taking the natives with us, we pulled up the anchor and started off. As we swung round a bend to the reach of the river where the trap was set, I felt a thrill of excitement, for it looked as if a cyclone had hit the trap. But then my heart sank, for the big branch to which we had fastened the wire noose was ripped from the tree. There was no crocodile in the remains of the trap. Dropping anchor, we went ashore to investigate. The fence had been completely demolished, and the mudbank ripped and torn out in chunks by great claws. Saplings had been bitten clean off, and young trees, evidently splintered by blows of a crocodile's tail, were smashed down into the mud. Then I noticed that both the log weight and the limb of the tree to which we had attached the wire noose had been dragged away, and were now firmly wedged between two big trees. The wire rope was still firmly attached to them, and led back into the gloom of the mangroves. Cautiously we followed it back amongst the trees, and there, at the full extent of the wire hawser, was a huge crocodile, with the noose firmly tightened about its middle. When we measured it later we found that it was eighteen feet six inches in length—not by any means a record, but eighteen-odd feet of crocodile looked awe-inspiring enough at such close quarters. A crocodile of this length is enormous in bulk, and a twelve-foot specimen is quite slim in comparison. This huge fellow had the girth of a big bullock.

Well, we had our crocodile, but I also wanted a motion picture, and it was quite impossible to do any filming in the gloom of the mangroves. As I circled round the trees behind our captive I felt quite safe, for the crocodile was tethered like a savage dog on a chain and could only go so far before the wire hawser would pull it up. Calling to the others to keep clear, I yelled loudly, and at the same time poked the crocodile vigorously with a long sapling, hoping to get it moving out into the open where the light would allow me to get the camera into action. Not an inch would it budge! In fact I began to think that the creature had killed itself by its strenuous attempts to get free. Cautiously I moved round to the side, and reaching forward with the stick, prodded it behind the front leg. This is a sensitive spot, and not heavily armoured. In fact, in the eye and behind the front leg are the two vulnerable spots for a rifle bullet. The poke having no result, I was practically certain that the brute was dead, but fortunately, before going any closer, I gave it another good jab with the stick.

Then—like an explosion—everything happened at once! The great jaws swung to the side with extraordinary rapidity and the stick was wrenched from my hand. At the same instant, the powerful tail thudded on the trunk of a tree alongside me. Instinctively I made a quick spring backwards, tripped on a mangrove root, and sat down heavily in the mud. The crocodile must have realized that it was too closely tethered to reach me, and made no move to follow up its advantage. As I sat there, I thought I must have imagined this sudden action, for the crocodile appeared to be in the same position and as immobile as when I had first seen it, but with this difference, that now, with jaws agape, it regarded me with a cynical smile. One glance at its baleful eye told me that it was merely sulking; there was still a big charge of dynamite in its mighty frame; I had merely tickled the percussion cap. We then tried with concerted effort to annoy the beast so that it would move into the open, but although it would snap fiercely from side to side, and lash its tail towards us, it would not leave its dark retreat amongst the mangroves. We decided to have breakfast, and think up other ways and means of enticing it out to have its portrait taken.

While we ate, the monster lay there with only the malignant glare from its eyes to tell us that it was not a stuffed museum specimen. As I bit into a damper fresh from the camp oven, I felt a smug satisfaction in the thought that my sixteen-stone frame was the largest in the party. So large is the throat of a crocodile of this size that it can swallow a small man in one piece, and so powerful are its digestive juices that the portion already engulfed commences to dissolve before the last part is gulped down.

By the end of breakfast we had made a decision. We would use the boat to tow the creature out. The first job was to make a noose from the end of the tow-line and get it over the beast's head. I got a forked sapling and, arranging a noose on it, gingerly approached our recalcitrant actor. But now I could not even make it lift its head up from the mud so that I could slip the noose into position. It just lay there, staring unwinkingly at me—and making me feel most uncomfortable. I began to wonder if a crocodile could hypnotize one as it is said the unwinking eye of a snake can hypnotize a bird.

One of the native boys in a spirit of scientific curiosity—or just plain devilment—caught up the cast-iron camp oven and flung it at the brute. In a flash the head swung round and snapped at the hurtling camp oven; the gleaming teeth crushed it, apparently without effort, and small pieces of cast-iron drippled from its jaws. Its head was just nicely placed for the noose, and in a flash I thrust the sapling forward and slipped the noose over. Immediately the sapling was torn from my hands, but this mattered not, for the noose was firmly in position. The natives took the other end of the lassoo to the boat, where it was soon tied fast, the engine started up, and the boat moved out into the river. The line tautened with a twang, but the crocodile just stayed put, as also did the boat, the propeller churning up the mud from the river bottom. For a few minutes the tug of war went on with neither side giving an inch; the boat might just as well have been moored to a wharf for all the effect it was having. I thought that another pound or two on the rope might do the trick, so, standing on the mudbank, I dug my feet in and put my full weight on the rope. That worked—a bit too well, for the crocodile came like a cork out of a bottle. In my desire to get it out to where photography was possible, I had quite lost sight of the fact that, should it make for me, I was sunk to the knees in mud, and without much chance of getting away. Not even that wonder horse, Phar Lap, could have made good time under such conditions. My first frenzied efforts to run sent me sprawling face down in the mud. A warning yell from my friend in the boat as he jumped for his rifle seemed to put extra speed into me. I lurched to my feet and broke into a desperate, stumbling run. There was a swish as the crocodile swung its tail towards me. Fortunately, it was only a glancing blow with the tip of its tail, for if it had struck me squarely it could have smashed both my legs like pipe-stems, but it was enough to send me spinning into the mud again. For some reason the brute did not attempt to seize me in its jaws. Probably bewildered by the yells of the natives, it ignored me and continued across the clearing until abruptly brought up short by the wire hawser. The sudden jolt caused it to erupt into furious action. Throwing its great bulk backwards until it almost stood on its hind-legs and tail, it lunged forward with such savage power that I doubted for a moment if the steel hawser could withstand the enormous strain; but again it was pulled up with a sudden jolt, and over and over the great brute rolled in the mud, bellowing in frenzied anger. Its claws ripped at the earth in its mad rage, and the powerful tail lashed from side to side; the ghastly jaws snapped together with a noise like the report of a gun. A post which had been used to build the fence was caught up, the jaws clamped down, and the post was flung aside bitten in half. Suddenly grasping the slack of the hawser in its jaws, the beast turned itself into a living corkscrew. Over and over it went, winding itself up in the steel rope, then without a moment's hesitation it reversed the action, unwound itself, took a fresh grip, and repeated the movement in the opposite direction. This twisting movement is natural to crocodiles, and is used by them when tearing flesh from their victims. Taking hold of a good mouthful, over they roll, wrenching the flesh out in one great piece.

By this time I had obtained a motion-picture record of the scene, but there was still much to be done if the brute was to be made captive for transport to a zoo. Despite the tremendous strength of the huge animal its frenzied struggles for freedom were tiring it, and soon it lay sulky and silent.

It would eventually have to be put in a long narrow cage for transport to a zoo, but it was impossible to carry such a large cage on a boat

The author emerges from the sea with his winged undersea camera.

Beauty and the beast are found together in the rivers where the
man-eating crocodiles lurk in tropical Australia.

small enough to negotiate the shallows in these crocodile rivers, so another method of making it captive had to be used. Chopping down a strong, straight young tree, we cleared the branches from its trunk. This gave us a stout pole a few feet more than the length of the crocodile. With this in readiness, we prepared another lassoo to fasten round the tail; the rope round its head had already been tied to a tree. Now with a long pole we manoeuvred the second lassoo over the tail. This was fastened to another tree on the opposite side of the clearing; once we had the two business ends of the brute under control, the remainder of the task was comparatively easy. The pole was laid along the back of the crocodile and, starting from the tip of the tail, we lashed ropes round it, binding it to the pole. This made a very efficient straitjacket, and it could neither swing its head nor lash its tail. With a rope round the snout and over the pole the beast was soon well muzzled, and lashings round the huge paws put them out of action. With our quarry safely trussed in this manner, the rest of the job was just plain hard work, and the four of us sweated and grunted as we manoeuvred the huge body down the bank and on to the boat; the first and hardest part of its journey to the zoo had been accomplished. What was more important to me—I had the film in the box! Now I could leave for the Gulf of Carpentaria to secure male and female specimens of *Crocodilus johnstoni*, the freshwater crocodile that lives far inland. This pair was also required for a zoo, and I wanted to film their capture.

The dry season was nearly over, and if the wet started early it would mean postponing the completion of my film, *Catching Crocodiles*, for another year. Once the rains started the flooding rivers would break their banks and, in the flat Gulf country, inundate the country over large areas. Small waterholes and lagoons become big lakes, and all motor vehicles just bog down.

Cairns was our nearest big port; so, our captive safely aboard and shaded under wet bags, we hauled up the anchor and, with a wave to the native boys happily stowing tobacco in their dilly-bags, we made down-river to the open sea and set sail for the south.

CHAPTER 3

NET RESULTS

THE grandeur of that sunrise! Great billowy clouds slowly changed from dusky red to gleaming gold. Then the sun shouldered the clouds aside and poured down a heat more appropriate to noontide, on a sea from the glassy surface of which the heat and glare ricocheted with increasing power. I have never viewed a grander dawn with more apprehension and disgust. Those great banks of clouds meant the wet season was perilously close. Speed was essential if any more work on crocodiles was to be done this year. Within an hour of our reaching Cairns the big salt-water crocodile was on the next step of its journey to the zoo, I had chartered a plane, and with only essential camera gear aboard I was up in the air and on my way to Normanton in the Gulf country.

In its glorious gold-mining yesterdays Normanton was the most prosperous town in the Far North. Now it is a dead town; but I almost resurrected it when I arrived there. Dashing into the sleepy bar of its main hotel--quite a good one, too—I called for drinks for all hands—there were but three customers—and commenced firing off questions.

"How long do you reckon before the wet sets in?"

"Anyone here got motor-trucks for hire?"

"Where do you get stores?"

"Are there many freshwater alligators in the lagoons this year?"

"Is there a good alligator trapper up here?"

One of the men finished the remainder of his hot beer—they had no ice in Normanton.

"George Smith's a beaut with 'gators," he drawled. "Makes bloody pets of 'em."

"Where can I find him?"

"Have another with me, mate, 'n I'll take you over to George's."

He ordered it. We drank it, and left.

The streets of sunbaked clay were cracked open with the long, rainless months, and our footsteps thudded on the earth with a peculiar hollow sound. The ground was so dry that the clay had a pleasant softness underfoot as if one were walking on cork; but hot! Without exaggeration, if one had broken an egg on the ground it would have fried within a very few minutes. And yet barefooted children driving milking goats passed us, and neither they nor the goats seemed to notice the burning heat. We crossed over the ornate iron gratings with their flourishing initials, N.C.C. The Normanton City Council had had those gratings specially made for all street crossings in the flamboyant gold-rush days. On past broad stone steps leading up from the wide street into—nothingness. Once one would have walked from the top step into the most flourishing emporium in the Far North. Now a hawk swooped at a chicken that was scratching in the dust. Crossing the sun-drenched vacant allotments, we came to a pioneer home of the early days, and there lounging on the veranda was George Smith.

We soon got down to details and George agreed to accompany me on the crocodile-trapping expedition.

"You get the stores over at B.P.'s," he said. "Enough for about a couple of days should do us."

"Two days?" I said doubtfully. "How do you make out that will be enough?"

"The wet will be on in about three or four days," said George, "and I'm going to be back here without having to swim home."

"About two days' stores, then," I said, rather hopelessly. "But I don't see much hope of getting any crocs. Do you want any ropes or pulley-blocks for the traps?"

George laughed at my dismal face.

"No, I'll take care of the gear. I'll meet you over at B.P.'s with two trucks and drivers. Don't you worry, I'll get them 'gators faster than you can get 'em into yer camera."

Well, it was nice to know that at least one of us was confident. Twenty minutes later he met me at B.P.'s, those ubiquitous purveyors of needles and anchors to the islands and to the Far North of Australia; an hour later we were well out from Normanton, speeding across salt-pans on our way to the freshwater lagoons and rivers.

The freshwater crocodile is a species peculiar to Australia. It is not a man-eater, its main diet being fish—although it enjoys a meal of warm-blooded meat if the animal is small enough to be tackled. These crocodiles seldom grow to a length greater than eight feet and are inoffensive if not molested or cornered. Then they become as ferocious as a savage dog, and attack in their efforts to escape. Nasty injuries can be inflicted by their long, slender jaws armed with teeth like rows of sharp nails. The powerful fore-paws have strong hooked claws that can maul a man most effectively.

Towards the end of the long dry season, when the rivers have ceased to flow and become merely a chain of isolated waterholes, the fresh-water crocodiles follow the dwindling water-supply and eventually crowd the deeper holes in the drying river beds. The fish have also congregated in these waterholes, and life for them takes on a new interest—if not a new lease. It is just one thing after another in the crowded pools.

Some distance ahead a thin line of trees meandering across the flat countryside showed where the river flowed in the wet season, and soon we pulled the trucks up in the shade of the trees. I got my camera out and we wended our way along the dry river bed. Cautiously I peeped round a bend in the river, then commenced setting up the movie camera. At least a dozen crocodiles were sunning themselves on the banks round a pool. I filmed a few feet of the peaceful scene, then asked George to fire his rifle into the air; after all, I wanted moving pictures, not sleeping crocodiles. At the report the crocodiles made a wild scramble down the bank and into the water.

Their speed on land is surprising; they have bodies much slimmer and lighter than the man-eating species, and are able to lift themselves completely off the ground and run on their four legs with the agility of a lizard. The salt-water crocodile is too heavy to do this, and its paws are used more like the paddles of a boat, causing the huge body to slide over the surface of the mud.

The pool was not still for long; as we watched the surface became dotted with little round knobs in groups of four, the two nearest in each group close together, and about a foot or so behind them two more knobs wider apart and a little larger. A glimpse through field-glasses resolved these little knobs into the nostrils and eyes of at least twenty to thirty crocodiles in that one pool! While floating at the surface they seldom show any more above water; even the ridges on their backs are submerged. We walked towards the pool and the knobs slowly sank. When we reached the bank there was not even a ripple on the surface. Before submerging, the crocodile closes its nostrils by means of a sphincter muscle, thus preventing the ingress of water.

Only a few hours ago we had sailed into the port of Cairns, and here I was hundreds of miles from there with some film already in the box and at least twenty actors waiting on the set. It is seldom that one gets such a break in wild-life photography. Often one goes for weeks without obtaining a foot of worthwhile film. Wild animals are natural actors, but not naturally actors.

A suggestion that we start building traps immediately did not meet with any enthusiasm. After taking a look at the sun, which was sinking behind the trees, George said that since it was much too late in the day to start work on any traps the best idea would be to bring the trucks here and make camp at the waterhole. This sounded a crazy idea to me, for not only were we wasting time by not building the traps, but would any crocodile be silly enough to come out of the water and walk into the traps—when they were built—while we were camped right alongside?

With a knowing smile George said, "I'll betcha a hundred quid that I'll have at least a dozen 'gators tied up on the bank here by midday tomorrow."

It was nice to know that one of us was so confident. We told the truck-drivers to bring the gear up to the waterhole and make camp.

We had seen many wild ducks flying overhead towards a big patch of reeds some distance back from the river. I asked George if there was water over there, and he told me that immediately after the wet season it was a small lake, but that now at the end of the dry it was merely a shallow, muddy lagoon where the wild water-fowl congregated. He suggested that we take the guns and get ducks for supper. As we made our way quietly through the reeds, I parted them, to look at the greatest number of wild ducks I have ever seen gathered in one spot. So massed were they that for a moment I thought there was no water at all; but as I watched I saw the birds performing the usual duck antic of standing on their heads in the water. There was the roar of a gun beside me, and I nearly did the same duck antic myself.

George had none of those ideas of sportsmanship whereby one picks one's bird off on the wing. He had come to get ducks for supper—and ducks he got, several with one barrel! Cartridges have to be transported hundreds of miles to the outback, and every cartridge counts. Not even the hungry hum of the mosquitoes kept me awake that night as I slept full-fed on wild duck.

After breakfast the next morning George still did not seem to be interested in traps, and when I remarked rather tersely that we'd better get on with the job he just grinned and suggested that I get my camera set up while he got the crocodiles. As I got my camera gear out, he started to unload one of the trucks, and before I had even set the camera up said that he was ready to catch the 'gators. There were no pulleys, no wire ropes, and no fences to be built. He had taken from the truck a long net, about eight feet deep and seventy-five feet in length, each end finished off with a stout pole, for all the world like a very deep, strong tennis net.

"No good for the 'gators you've been trapping," he said. "Those big fellows would rip it to ribbons, but it'll hold these all right."

Naturally I thought that he would set it as one does a fishing net, across the waterhole, and wait for the crocodiles to mesh in it; but no—that was much too slow for George. Taking the net to the end of the waterhole, he stationed the two truck-drivers with the pole at one end of the net, then, paying the net out as he went, took the other end across the river bed until it was stretched taut in the shallows across the end of the waterhole. Calling to the men on the opposite bank to keep pace with him, he started moving slowly along the bank on the other side of the pool, the net sinking deeper as the shallows were passed. For a time nothing happened, then in the part of the waterhole not yet traversed by the net the surface was broken in all directions by little knobs of nostrils and eyes. The crocodiles, evidently curious to see what was going on, had come up to investigate. As the net approached them, they did not submerge slowly as before: it was now a case of "slam the hatch and crash-dive". George called to his mates to hold tight while he dug one end of his pole into the ground and prepared to pull back on it with all his weight. Some of the crocodiles decided to run the gauntlet and charged the net. The men rocked and staggered as they took the force of the impact; they looked

Kitty and Noel Monkman, usually an expedition of two, have for many years explored the Great Barrier Reef and the tropical jungles of Australia in search of wild life for the movie camera. (Photo: Fred Carew.)

Kitty (the author's wife) and the caravan.

Kitty, an enthusiastic shell collector, shows her latest treasures to her husband, Noel.

as if they were being buffeted by an invisible opponent. Then all was still again. Once again the surface was dotted by eyes and nostrils, but this time at the far end of the pool a long way from the net.

Again the net was slowly dragged onward through the water, and as it approached the crocodiles once more disappeared. There must have been a concerted rush under water, and the men staggered while they hung on to their poles like grim death. George was dragged to his knees in his efforts to hold fast, and leaving the camera I rushed to his assistance. The pole kicked and jumped in our hands like a live thing, and I felt as if my arms were being dragged out of their sockets and then allowed to snap back again. It was a grim tussle for a few minutes, then once more everything was quiet in the net, but the far end of the pool was heaving and bubbling like a boiling mud-pool. As the net moved forward the water fairly churned: it was not only eyes and nostrils now but the lashing tails and scrambling bodies of the crocodiles. Inexorably the net approached them: again came a concerted rush, and again we battled to hold the net round the struggling saurians. Some won their way to freedom under the net, for here and there in the part of the pool already dragged we could see their snouts and eyes appearing. Although the net still jerked and jumped in our hands, we commenced to move on again until we reached the shallows at the far end, which was now a squirming mass of crocodiles climbing over each other's backs and making wild dashes from one side of the net to the other in their efforts to escape. The two poles of the net were now brought together, completing a circle round the struggling animals. Slowly, inch by inch, we dragged the net from the water and on to the bank. Several crocodiles were making them- selves helpless by snapping at the net and rolling over and over in the usual crocodile manner, winding the net in a ball round their snouts, thus putting their jaws completely out of action. As we sank panting on the bank I wondered whether we or the crocodiles were the more exhausted. They reminded me of a lot of onions in a string bag, but there was a decided difference in the odour. Crocodiles have special glands under the front legs and in the groin that give off an unpleasant, musky smell. Sitting there I counted our captives. We had secured thirteen in one haul! In size they ranged from three feet to between six and seven feet; the largest specimen was nearly eight feet, an unusually large example of its species.

George said that he could do as good, or better, in the next haul; but jubilantly packing my film away I said that there would be no need for another haul because I already had more than I needed. I had hoped to secure only a pair for the zoo, but now I could make doubly sure with two pairs.

The next job was to get them tied up for transport. This did not present the difficulties encountered when tying up the huge man-eaters. With the crocodiles still tangled up, the snouts were worked through the meshes until they protruded through the net. It was while doing this that I discovered an interesting thing about these crocodiles, which also applies in a degree to the big estuarine species. The muscles that open the jaws are comparatively weak, and the enormous power can only be brought to bear when closing the jaws, which were then snapping viciously with a sound like castanets. The moment they closed, the opportunity was seized to grasp the snouts, which were fairly easy to keep closed with a firm grip of one hand. The crocodiles were then effectively muzzled with a rope lashed round the snout.

Another point of interest is the tongue. There is no organ that can be protruded from the mouth, and where one would expect to see a tongue there is merely the smooth unbroken lining of the lower jaw. Evolution has found another use for the crocodile's tongue: it has been so modified that it no longer fulfills the usual functions of a tongue, but is used as a valve to close the throat against the inrush of water when the animal submerges or seizes its prey under water.

Once the jaws were muzzled only the claws and tails had to be watched. One man would firmly grasp a lashing tail and draw one of the crocodiles slowly from the net. The crocodile would try to avoid being dragged backward by digging its claws into the ground. This gave a perfect opportunity to slip a lashing on the paws and bind them close to the animal's body. They were then put in the back of the trucks where they wriggled round frantically, but could not climb out.

As my pub friend had said, "George Smith's a beaut with 'gators."

Three of the captives were sent on to the zoo by boat from Norman-ton, but the big one was such a fine specimen that I did not like to risk it on a long sea voyage, so put it in a crate and arranged for a plane to fly us both to Cairns.

The crocodile made no fuss as we took off, but lay quiet in its crate. Flying over Cape York we had to climb high over gathering rain-clouds. Hooray! Thanks to George's unorthodox trapping methods I had beaten the wet.

The rarefied air at this high altitude, however, did not at all meet with the crocodile's approval; it kicked up the devil of a fuss and ripped at the crate with its claws, while lashing about furiously with its armoured tail. It had every reason to feel uneasy, for I have no doubt that this was the first time since the evolution of the crocodile that one of its species had been a plane passenger.

Uneasily the pilot glanced back at the crate. The crocodile was now trying to push its head out through the bars, and there was a sound of tearing wood as its claws raked viciously at the wooden crate.

Turning to me, the pilot said, "Can you fly a plane?"

"No," I replied.

"Well," he said, "this seems a pretty good time for you to learn. If that pal of yours gets out of the box I'm going out on the wing."

CHAPTER 4

CARAVAN AND CAMERA

WHILE awaiting my return to the south from the crocodile country, my wife, Kitty, had been fitting out a motor caravan for our next expedition. And while I revelled in hot showers, clean clothes, fresh fruit and vegetables, and a welcome respite from leeches and mosquito and sandfly bites, Kitty was thoroughly happy planning her household arrangements for caravan life. With great pride she showed me her built-in kerosene cooker, a sink with a shiny water tap above it, built-in bunks and store cupboards, dainty window curtains, and all the other feminine trimmings so essential to make a contented housewife: and as a crowning glory there was a nook that became a shower-room. I must admit that my main interest was a good engine and the arrangements necessary to turn the caravan into a darkroom, with a solid built-in table to bear the weight, without tremors, of my optical bench for photo-micrographic work. When completed the caravan was quite a roomy home and laboratory, built on a two-ton-truck chassis, with a large trailer carrying the engine and generator for the electric arcs and camera motors, and the extra petrol and water required for traversing desert country. We planned to wander through many seldom-visited parts of Australia, and stored away in the trailer were spare engine parts and rolls of coconut matting to spread over the sandy places we knew we should encounter. Without that matting we should never have completed our journey: we should have been forced to abandon the caravan, sunk deep in the sand, and to attempt the impossible task of walking back to civilization.

We hear a great deal about the "boundless ocean", but somehow I have never felt the immensity of the ocean to the extent that I have realized the immensity of Australia. Perhaps the reason lies in the boundary set by the horizon at sea. The curve of the surface of the sea completely hides a small island only four of five miles away, and Omar's inverted bowl is a very large blue bowl certainly, but it is limited also by that same finite boundary of horizon. Our caravan gave us a new concept of distance; in the outback we have travelled until nightfall without seeming much nearer to the foothills of mountain ranges we had seen blushing crimson in the light of dawn. In the uninhabited, unfenced outback one travels as does the mariner, by marking out a course on the map, and steering by compass. There are few roads, and no signposts, but to the naturalist the country is well populated and our cameras were kept busy with a wealth of fascinating motion-picture material. Some of our film stars even forced themselves upon us. We were filming the life history of a Mutillid Wasp. The name records that science has noticed a peculiarity of this insect, for the female looks as if she had been cruelly mutilated by having her wings torn off: but this is a natural condition, she is born without wings. This is not the case with the males, whose flight is strong and swift as they search for their earthbound mates.

I was engrossed in filming the wingless female digging her nest in the bank by a small lagoon when suddenly I felt a sharp pain on the cheek followed by several quick stabs on the neck. Glancing up from the camera I found a swarm of small wasps buzzing angrily round me. The camera had been set up under a tree where a colony of paper-wasps had built their home. Bee nets provided us with protection and the camera was soon at work on the annoyed colonists. The nest of these wasps is well constructed, waterproof, and warm; the only entrance is underneath, in order that the rains may not enter the nest.

It took man many thousands of years before he learnt to make paper from wood, but these little wasps have known the secret for ages. They chew the wood to a pulp, and fashion from it sheets of paper with which they build their comfortable nests. Whilst the months remain warm and sunny the wasp community flourishes and each insect carries out its allotted task. But with the coming of the colder months this routine is suddenly upset. Instinct tells the workers that a shortage of food is approaching. The wasps attempt to find a solution to the problem of supply and demand, and the worker wasps, which up till then have been assiduously tending and feeding the larvae, commence to reduce the number of mouths to be fed by tearing the helpless grubs from their cells and casting them from the nest to perish. Unhappily this drastic remedy is not successful; the old queen and the workers soon die, to be followed by the young males, who perish shortly after impregnating the young queens. These young queens keep alive through the winter months by becoming cannibals and eat the remainder of the wasp larvae in the nest, and so survive to become the mothers of the next year's communities.

Wasps and bees have many similar characteristics, but when I made the film *The Winged Empress* I showed how cleverly the honey-bees had solved this problem of winter, with its diminished food-supplies, by storing waxen cupboards with honey. As the winter months went slowly by the usual busy life of the hive was almost at a standstill. The queen had ceased to lay, and the bees were gathered together in a drowsy, sluggish mass. But food was there in plenty, and the honey was passed from one bee's tongue to the other through all that sleepy mass, until the warmth of spring and the fragrance of the opening flowers roused the bees from their lethargy.

It is possible that I have been guilty of a scientific misdemeanour in stating that the bees had *cleverly* solved a problem the solution of which had evaded the wasps. Science considers it a heinous crime to attribute to insects the ability to reason or to think things out as we humans do. And yet the longer I worked on *The Winged Empress* film the more difficult it was to believe that the motivating force behind the habits of the bees was merely blind instinct. When they stored their honey they behaved like skilled chemists and put a tiny drop of formic acid into it to prevent fermentation. If they found the honey too watery they put on special gangs of workers to evaporate the water by fanning the air over the open honey-pots with their rapidly vibrating wings. My gravest doubt as to instinct being a satisfactory explanation was aroused when the queen of a hive I was filming died. While she had lived everything had gone ahead smoothly, and the bees went contentedly about their duties. With her death, confusion and a seeming panic took possession of the workers. Work ceased, and they ran about the hive in an aimless, dazed fashion. The death of the queen can cause the extinction of the hive unless there is a baby queen who will take her place. In this hive there was no young queens. Gradually the aimless confusion died down, and the bees commenced their duties again. What was the explanation? Without a queen the work was useless; why collect nectar from the blossoms and convert it into honey? Why continue making beeswax for comb that would never be filled with its golden store? Without the queen mother there could be no eggs to bring forth a new generation to eat the honey.

But soon a young queen was once more reigning in the hive. The workers had used a worker egg laid by their dead queen, and had transformed it into a queen. When the old queen was laying she had moved over the comb, laying two kinds of eggs in three different kinds of comb. When laying in worker cells she laid an egg that could develop into either a queen, or a worker; in the larger drone cells a drone egg was deposited; and if she had laid a queen-egg it would have been in the special cells constructed for queen babies. Since she had not bequeathed a queen-egg to the hive, the worker bees had developed a new queen by feeding a grub that had hatched from a worker egg with a special food; this special food develops the sex organs of what would have been an ordinary worker, making a perfect female. Such marvels would seem to demand a more satisfying explanation than "mere instinct".

Having decided that the insects must be reasoning creatures, we were baffled by the utter stupidity of a mud-dauber wasp we photographed. This wasp collected clay from the bank of the river to construct the cradles for her future babies. If the clay became too dry for satisfactory manipulation she would bring a drop of water from the river and moisten it until it suited her requirements. This seemed a very sensible procedure, and again it seemed science was too sweeping with its accent on instinct. After many trips for mud and water she completed a cell, then caught a spider and put it into the cell together with a wasp egg, so that when the young wasp hatched it would find a spider ready to be eaten. While the wasp worked we had seen a small lizard poke its head out from behind a nearby piece of bark. The bright eyes watched the activities of the wasp with interest. When the wasp placed the spider in the cell she started to seal the opening with mud. The little lizard watched her as she flew between the nest and the river collecting her pellets of mud. As she left for another load the lizard suddenly darted to the nest pulled the spider out of the cell, and was safely behind the piece of bark before the wasp returned from the river. As the lizard made a leisurely meal of the spider the wasp continued sealing up the empty cell. There was not the slightest doubt that the sharp eyes of the wasp could see that the cell was now empty, but she had reached the stage where instinct compelled her to carry out a pre-ordained routine, and she went ahead with her useless toil. The little lizard gobbled up the last of the spider and returned to its sly watching. Time after time the lizard stole the spiders as the cells were being sealed, and the stupid wasp continued with her absurd task of sealing up the empty cells. No—there is no intelligence, it *is* instinct; but wait—the lizard was clever!

The caravan had lurched and ground its way up the rugged side of a mountain range, and at the summit the overheated engine cooled off while we looked down on a huge encampment on the plain beneath us. There seemed enough bell tents to shelter a bigger army than Australia could put into the field. As we drew near, the tents resolved themselves into white-ant nests rising from the plain to a a height of up to nine or ten feet. There were hundreds of them, each only a few yards apart on that scorching plain. Although the scene was wriggling and wavering in the heat shimmer, we made camp and prepared to include something of the life of the white-ants in our film, *Ants and Their Antics*. The white-ant is really not an ant at all, but a termite, and it is a distant relative of the cockroach. Considering the small size of these insects, even the most towering skyscrapers built by man lose something of their wonder when compared with their gigantic architectural achievements. These spacious ant-hills could not be built without the closest co-operation between the individuals of the community, which is split up into several different kinds of termites: the tiny indefatigable workers, the soldiers with their massive heads and powerful jaws, the males or consorts of the queen, and the queen herself.

In the design of the termite social system there is something of the brave new world of Aldous Huxley's novel. He imagined a future world where human babies would be developed in test tubes, and would be treated in such fashion during their earlier development that they would reach adulthood fitted and useful for but one rôle in the human community. The individuals that make up each termite community are not only physically designed to carry out their particular work most efficiently, but are also mentally or psychologically adapted for it. A worker termite is a timid creature and quickly gives way to confusion and panic if danger threatens the community. All it desires is to be left in the dark—it shuns the light—and allowed to work itself quietly to death for the common good of the community. Not so the soldier termite, for danger brings out the very qualities that have been developed in it for the protection of the community: savagery and the dogged courage that makes it prefer to die at its post rather than surrender. We found this when cutting with a hacksaw through the stone-like wall of the nest. The soldier termites would rush to the gaps made in the inner passageways and barricade the openings with their huge heads, the formidable mandibles clashing with rage. Nothing would make them retreat; they bit savagely at whatever we put within their reach. Protected by these valiant warriors, the timid workers built barricades behind their soldiers and sealed the passageways up, leaving the soldiers with no possible hope of falling back if outnumbered or outfought.

It is the duty of the queen termite to produce replacements for individuals lost by warfare, overwork, sickness, or old age. Since there are hundreds of thousands of worker termites in a community, with approximately one soldier to every five workers, the job of keeping up such numbers requires efficiency on the part of the queen. To attain this extraordinary efficiency the queen has forgone the ability to move about, and has developed into a mere egg-laying machine.

Deep in the heart of the termite city was the royal chamber where she was confined—in both senses of the word. She was a grotesque-looking insect, with a tiny head and thorax like a small black bead stuck on the end of her huge sausage-like body. She was designed only for the laying of eggs, and in that one job she was super-efficient. The workers were in ceaseless attendance collecting her never-ending stream of eggs and transporting them to the brood chambers. In these nurseries, deep in the inner chambers of the nest, the miraculous development of the required types of individuals was carried out, but how the wonder was performed baffled the utmost efforts of our cameras.

It was a welcome relief to leave the parched plains and the sand of desert areas as we crossed over another mountain range and came to the coastal regions of Cape York. Following the course of a swiftly flowing river we came to a pleasant grassy glade shaded by trees. It was a lovely spot, so I pulled up under a big tree and we prepared to make our camp. Almost as soon as we got out of the caravan we were bitten on the legs, and then on the neck and face. Ants were not only swarming on us from the ground, but falling from the trees. The ants on the grass swarmed straight up our legs and, by some sort of insect radio, the ones in the trees above seemed to know of our presence: instead of crawling down the trunks of the trees to join their comrades in the grass they dropped down from the branches above us like a green rain. The moment they landed—in went their nippers! It felt like the stab of a red-hot needle. Any attempt to brush them off failed; they would not loosen the bulldog grip of their jaws, and the brushing only knocked the bodies off and left the heads with the nippers still buried in our skins. They were savage little beasties, so we moved camp a short distance away, then returned with the cameras to study these pugnacious midgets.

In the trees were what looked like a number of green footballs, which we found to be made of leaves most ingeniously joined together. With a stick I tapped lightly on one of these structures, and out from tiny doorways poured an army of green ants. So thickly did they cluster upon the football of leaves that it was completely hidden, and looked as if it were made of green fur. The infuriated little house-holders stood up on tiptoe as they sprang from side to side in short, angry leaps.

This was a nest of the green tree-ants of tropical Australia, and for weeks we remained camped near the glade while we watched and filmed these little green warriors. When we filmed the life of the honey-bees we had found they were a gracious community that soon became accustomed to us. As long as we were quiet and moved smoothly and slowly among them they let us take quite outrageous liberties, and rarely showed any resentment. This was not the case with the green ants, which most viciously resented any prying into their domestic arrangements. Although we had worked without any protection from the bees, I found it necessary when filming the green ants to bind the legs of my trousers, put gloves on with my sleeves pushed inside them, and tie a piece of mosquito-netting round my hat, tucking the end of it inside the collar of my shirt. The vicious little beasts would even swarm up the tripod legs and bite the camera!

However, it was well worth all the discomfort, for their life history was most interesting.

Only the queen ants and their bridegrooms are winged, and leaving the nests where they were born they go on a honeymoon flight. Having mated, the female ant leaves her bridegroom for ever and, alone, she undertakes not only the care of a family but the founding of a city. She begins to lay her eggs. The first ants to hatch from these eggs find a mother too busy with egg-laying to give them a great deal of attention, so these ants suffer from malnutrition, and accordingly do not attain the size that they would if they had been properly fed. These dwarfed ants take upon themselves the care of their younger sisters, for, as with the honey-bees, the workers among the ants are undeveloped females. Assiduously they forage for food so that their younger sisters, being properly fed, now outgrow their nurses. Now they in turn take up a task, perhaps the most wonderful of the many wonderful things ants are capable of. Upon them rests the responsibility of building a city. Shoulder to shoulder they line up along the edge of a growing leaf; other ants then walk forward over their bodies and are gripped firmly about the waist by the jaws of the ones on the edge of the leaf. More ants follow over the bodies of those already hanging pendant from the edge of the leaf, until a living chain of ants swings out into space like acrobats hanging from a trapeze. These long chains start swinging like a pendulum of a clock until the ant at the end of the chain is able to grasp an adjacent leaf in its jaws. Straining mightily, the tiny insects draw the leaves towards each other by shortening the living chains until the edges of the leaves meet. So far, so good, but how now are the leaves to be permanently fastened?

This problem is solved in a most remarkable manner. As we watched we saw an ant come striding through the workers with something gripped in its jaws. It was a little white grub, an immature baby ant still in the larval form. Taking its place astride the two leaves, this worker ant began to wave the baby rhythmically from side to side. It appeared to be some kind of mystic rite; but surely they did not require a living sacrifice to commemorate the building of a city! As the waving went on, the tropic sun caught a gleam from a misty something that was appearing across the leaves. This required closer inspection, and with the aid of a magnifying glass the wonder was

33

revealed. The worker pressed one end of the baby ant against the leaf, then gave it a sharp nip as a signal for it to commence work, whereupon the baby began to spin a fine silken thread. This thread should really be used in the weaving of its own cradle or cocoon, but necessity forces its elder sisters to use the baby as a needle and thread with which to sew the home together. Occasionally an ant holding the edges of the leaves together with the grip of its jaws is too obstinate to relinquish its hold; no matter, the ant who is doing the sewing just stitches the body of her foolish sister into the fabric to remain there to die: an incident rather reminiscent of the ancient custom of walling up human sacrifices.

No sooner does one baby run out of silk than a new infant is brought into use. Leaf after leaf is stitched together in this way until the structure is completed, and mother, daughters, eggs, and babies are safely housed in the nest.

But still more work remains to be done. There are outhouses to be built for the "cattle" these ants keep: insects that give off a sweet fluid called honey-dew, of which the ants are particularly fond. To prevent these herds from straying, more leaves are sewn together until the captive herds are safely fenced in. The ants care for these herds just as carefully as a human farmer cares for his cattle, and if the fodder becomes exhausted on one tree the ants remove their "insect cattle" to fresh pastures where there are plenty of leaves to feed on.

We witnessed a most puzzling example of insect instinct—or was it intelligence? One night we were returning to where we had made camp close to a small creek. We had been experiencing a heat-wave with the thermometer registering up to 110 degrees in the shade. Day followed day with a burning sun, with not even a breeze to temper the scorching heat. Nor did evening bring much relief, for with the setting of the sun the parched earth assumed the role of heat-giver and poured out its stored heat of the day into the still night air. This particular night differed in no respect from any of the other nights; it was hot, but calm and peaceful, with a full moon lighting up the countryside. As we neared the caravan we saw what appeared to be a black rope running from underneath it and stretching in a straight line across the ground for about a hundred yards. Upon investigation this apparent rope proved to be a long line of ants. They were abandoning a nest on the bank of the creek, and were carrying their eggs, larvae, and bits and pieces of furnishings to another nest. The ants appeared to be in a desperate hurry, and a procession of "empties" was streaming back to the nest to load up again. Before the moon set, the evacuation of the old nest was completed. We watched this activity in wonderment, for there appeared to be no reason for it. The next day rain fell, and the small creek soon flooded over its banks and completely submerged the nest the ants had just vacated. What strange sense could have warned the ants of the flood to come? They possessed no barometers or other instruments of the meteorologist. The more one watches ants the more one marvels at the strange similarity between man-made civilization and that of the ants. While one accepts the opinion of science that instinct, not intelligence, guides the doings of these little creatures, one feels compelled to reserve at least the right to wonder.

With the last scenes of *Ants and Their Antics* completed, we packed up the undeveloped negative and posted it from the nearest post-office to a southern film laboratory to be processed.

Then came a telegram from the south:

FIRE IN LABORATORIES REGRET INFORM YOU ALL YOUR NEGATIVE ANTS AND ANTICS DESTROYED STOP SUGGEST YOU RETAKE

Retake! That picture had portrayed incidents in the life histories of many species of ants; we had travelled over two thousand miles during its production; weeks of painstaking work had gone into it; there were scenes we could never hope to. . . . Oh, what was the use? Apparently they thought we were working in a studio where we could put on the call board:

CALL FOR RETAKES

Scenes	Complete life histories.
Stars	Miss Ant and Bridegroom.
	Make-up—8 a.m.
	On set—9 a.m.
Extras	Worker and Soldier ants.
	Make-up—7 a.m.
	On set—8 a.m.

35

CHAPTER 5

THE DEMON IN THE PIT

THE thunder of the tropical downpour caused us no more inconvenience than the necessity of raising our voices above the din of the beating rain. We had experienced such storms many times, and knew that our camp was weatherproof. But our guest from the city was rather worried.

"I'm afraid the rain must be coming into my tent," she said. "It's making pits all over the floor."

Kitty smiled; she had seen thousands of similar pits in the inland where there had not been even a shower of rain for years.

"Those pits aren't made by the raindrops," she replied.

Taking a length of cotton and a knitting needle, she fashioned a tiny fishing rod, observing as she baited the cotton with a scrap of raw meat, "A fly or an ant is really the best bait, but they'll bite at this."

Our guest looked bewildered.

"What'll bite?"

"The little demons in the pits. This is how we caught our actors when we made a film about them."

Carefully the bait was lowered until it touched the edge of one of the circular pits in the sand. A few dislodged grains rolled down the side of the pit to the bottom.

"It's more like a volcano than a pit now!" said our guest excitedly. "It's throwing up sand!"

The bait was allowed to roll down with the sand grains, and immediately a pair of pincer-like jaws struck—a quick flick of the knitting needle—and the demon lay in the palm of Kitty's hand. Cautiously our visitor poked the insect with her finger.

"What is it?" she asked. "It seems to be dead."

"It's an ant-lion," said Kitty, as she put it down on the sand, "and it's not dead, it's only shamming."

During our film work on this insect we had found that it invariably feigned death when captured. It is hard to understand this peculiarity; under natural circumstances it is difficult to imagine a situation where such a ruse would be needed to protect the ant-lion from an enemy. In fact, I have seen this habit cause the death of one that could quite easily have escaped. When putting some captured specimens in a box, one dropped to the ground. Knowing that it would sham dead for a short time I left it there while putting the others away. Bending to pick it up, I saw that an ant had seized one of the legs of the ant-lion and was hanging on like a bulldog. The ant-lion was lying on its back apparently dead. As I watched, another ant arrived and seized another leg. In a few minutes the unfortunate insect had an ant clinging to each of its legs, and only then did it decide to stop shamming dead and do something. But it was too late, for other ants were arriving and soon the ant-lion made a meal for them.

As we watched the specimen Kitty had placed back on the sand it suddenly came to life again. With a quick movement of its head it flicked itself over and was right side up. Immediately it started digging backwards into the sand, and in a few seconds was out of sight. A retrogressive little beast is the ant-lion; it must always travel backwards through life, for so huge are its jaws that, one might say, it trips over its teeth if it attempts to walk forward. Ant-lions always seek for a dry place in which to make their pits, which dimple the ground at the entrance to caves, or in the shelter of overhanging ledges on cliffs, or indeed anywhere where they can find dry, dusty ground or sand where the beating rains cannot break down their carefully constructed food traps or pits.

The insect makes this pit by walking backwards in a descending spiral. As it descends, it uses the flat back of its head like a shovel with which to toss the unwanted sand well away from the inverted cone of its deepening pit. The symmetry of the conical pit is remarkable. From a circular top about an inch or two in diameter the sand slopes smoothly down to a point about an inch below the level of the ground. The ant-lion buries its body under the sand at the bottom of the pit, but often leaves its head and jaws protruding in readiness to grasp any unwary insect that may attempt to make its way across the shifting sands on the treacherous sides of the trap. If the ant-lion is completely buried at the foot of the trap, the sand grains dislodged by an insect within the trap, warn it that a victim is almost within reach. The head and jaws of the little demon are immediately thrust up from the bottom of the pit and, quickly taking a load of sand on the back of its head, it gives a flick that sends the sand hurtling up the side of the pit, knocking the struggling victim from its precarious foothold and starting a miniature landslide. This carries the hapless insect down to the waiting jaws, which immediately fasten into the body of the creature and draw it beneath the sand, where all its juices are sucked out. The meal completed, the ant-lion again protrudes its head from the bottom of the pit and, with the same quick flick it used for throwing sand, sends the emptied carcass of its victim hurtling right out of the pit to fall on the ground some distance away from the trap: no warning is left at the entrance of the peril that lurks beneath.

There comes a day when the ant-lion is no longer interested in capturing ants; it lies quiescent beneath the sand and changes from its baby larval stage into a pupa, from which, in due course, emerges a beautiful lacewing, *Myrmeleon*. It resembles a fragile edition of the dragonfly, delicately coloured, with iridescent gauzy wings. This new raiment is its bridal dress, and the mating urge is strong within it. Its mate found, it enjoys a brief honeymoon, lays it eggs, and dies. From those eggs come forth the demons of the pit. Now here is a very remarkable thing about the childhood of this lovely *Myrmeleon*: although its life as an adult fly is very brief, in its immature stage as an ant-lion the less it eats the longer it lives. When meals are plentiful the ant-lion feeds bounteously and grows mightily, and yet it might truthfully be said that in doing so it digs its grave with its own "teeth", for the insect at this carnivorous stage of its life history is but a child, and the more it eats the more rapidly it grows up. If no victims enter the trap it can exist for many months without any food. If prey is scarce, and meals reach it only by dribs and drabs, it develops very slowly and may remain an ant-lion for several years before changing into its winged, adult form.

It is these queer life histories that make the filming of insects so fascinating: the children of the insects often do not resemble their parents in the slightest degree. It must have taken careful observation by the early naturalist to discover that the repulsive maggot crawling in filth was the child of the common blowfly. And how startling an

The head and jaws of the little demon are thrust up from
the bottom of the pit. (Photo-micrograph.)

Top left: The tiny bee bites out a little cave
about the size of a grain of wheat.

Bottom left: The little mother lies in her tomb.

Top right: A miraculous change is slowly taking place.

Bottom right: The young bee awakens at the call of spring.

(All from the film *The Cliff Dweller.*)

experience it is to watch an ugly, grotesque creature crawl up a reed from a stagnant pool, and then to see the back of this ugly creature suddenly split open, and from it emerge the graceful, swift dragonfly. The baby of the dragonfly was, until it emerged from the water, a fierce, carnivorous creature, preying upon the other creatures that lived in the water. When an inhabitant of the underwater world, it was a rapacious masked bandit. The mask not only covered its face, but was used as a terrible weapon with which to seize its prey. This mask fits snugly over the face while the young dragonfly is at rest or waiting in the depths of the pool for a victim. When some unsuspecting pond inhabitant approaches close enough, the mask is lifted from the young dragonfly's face and flashes out on a hinged arm, scooping up the victim and conveying it to the waiting jaws. Who would suspect that this repulsive, nightmarish-looking creature living in the depths of the pools, was the child of the iridescent dragonfly scorching the air above the sunlit streams?

Many insects in their larval stage or babyhood are ghoulish creatures, and in some cases the parents are not blameless. The common spider-hunting wasp is one of these. Alert, with quick, springy movements and antennae a-tremble, she moves in search of a spider. One of her intended victims, seeing her approach, seems to know well that with the wasp comes death, for the spider makes a dash for cover. Like a flash the wasp pursues. Realizing that it cannot match that flashing speed, the spider halts and wheels around, gallantly prepared to fight it out. It assumes a fearsome, fighting attitude, with strong, hairy legs upheld, thorax and head lifted well back, and its poison fangs open; the spider is ready to do or die. Almost invariably it is to die, for the wasp moves like lightning. But she is no rough and tumble fighter who overwhelms her opponent with smashing blows or rending fangs; the victory is won with the cool calculation of a scientist in a laboratory. Her weapon is the finest of hypodermic syringes—her sting. Nor is this sting plunged haphazard into the body of her opponent. She seeks not to kill, but to paralyse by striking at a nerve ganglion and injecting the poison that will cause a living death to the spider. Not for herself but for her unborn children is she seeking a meal, and it is necessary that the meat be fresh and alive when they partake of it, hence there must be no killing stroke, but paralysis and—let us hope—anaesthesia.

It would be distasteful to think that the spider remains conscious through what is to come. The wasp now drags the inert body of the spider to her nest, or it might be more truly called a cradle, for she has built it for the young wasps-to-be. An egg is laid upon the body of the spider, and from it soon hatches a grub that burrows into the living meat. Deep into the living spider's body it eats its way: but, guided by an uncanny instinct, it does not gnaw at the vital organs until all the rest is consumed. Only then will it eat the vital parts, thus bringing death to the paralysed spider. The baby wasp has fed on the living meat during its whole babyhood, and inside the empty shell of the spider the wasp grub now pupates, finally emerging from the husk of the spider ready to fly out into the world, meet its mate, and commence the life cycle again.

Another insect has gone even a step farther in providing food for its babies. So fragile and dainty are these little insects that they have been given the appropriate name of "fairy flies". When a lad I was privileged to be the first naturalist to discover the existence of certain species of Australasian fairy flies. I well remember the look of horror on my mother's face when she first discovered her son lying in the grass, squinting horribly, while he aimlessly waved a hair pulled out of the dog's tail in front of those squinting eyes. I had learnt to keep my eyes in focus at only a few inches' distance, and would lie with my face in the grass until a tiny fairy fly floated into view, when a light touch with the hair, which had been dipped in dilute gum, resulted in the capture of the fairy fly. This explanation did not satisfy my mother, whose unaided eyes were still unable to see the fairy fly, until under my microscope she saw the hair, which now looked like a sturdy perch, with a fairy fly as big as a bird adhering to it. Actually, so small are some of the fairy flies, that four of them abreast could pass through the eye of a needle.

The mother fairy fly searches until she finds a larger insect busy laying its eggs. She awaits her opportunity, then settles on the eggs and, piercing the shell with her ovipositor, lays her egg inside the egg of the other insect. This does not prevent the other insect's egg from hatching, but when the caterpillar emerges from its shell it carries the egg of the fairy fly buried in its body. At this stage the tiny egg does not inconvenience the caterpillar, which commences to eat leaves and grow big and fat. Then, deep within the well-fed body, the fairy fly grub emerges from its egg, and commences to feed upon the living tissues of the caterpillar, in which it pupates and eventually emerges as an adult fairy fly. As it dries its dainty wings in the sunshine, it stands upon the dead body of the caterpillar, for, like the wasp baby, the fairy fly grub has dined upon the vital organs of its host.

But not all baby insects behave so fiendishly. Perhaps the saddest life history I filmed was that of a primitive Australian bee. I was introduced to this little bee by Mr Tarlton Rayment, naturalist, novelist, artist, and an outstanding authority on bees. With the infinite patience of the true naturalist he had discovered and worked out the life history of this survival of the stone age ancestor of our modern honeybee. Its life story was so appealing that I could not rest content until I had preserved it in celluloid. But I had not realized the difficulties we were to encounter in making a motion picture of such a subject. Since most of the life of this bee is spent in a tunnel in the ground, the photographic problems were multitudinous. Opportunities had to be seized, when the bee was supping at the flowers, to cut, then face her tunnel with glass. Since the worker toils in darkness, the light had to be completely blocked from this glass-fronted tunnel with a screen of black velvet. Much of her activity continues throughout the night, which necessitated arc lights with cooling troughs being placed to shine on to the tunnel in the stone. The black velvet screen could not be removed for more than scanty seconds, during which only a few feet of film could be secured. The intense light in her normally dark tunnel would soon frighten the little worker and she would cease work. If the light was not turned off immediately, she showed signs of uneasiness, then there would be a sudden scurry—and the tunnel would be empty.

Bee after bee gave up her attempt to cope with our interference with her normal life, and, with another actress, work had to commence all over again. Each failure, however, was a partial success, because only thus were the problems solved. After many months of constant endeavour we completed the film *The Cliff Dwellers*, the life story of the tiny prehistoric bee that lives, loves, and dies today as did its ancestors thousands of years ago.

From such beginnings came the evolution of the modern hive of the honey-bee with its thousands of workers and great stores of honey: a close parallel to man's cave-dwelling ancestors, and the thronging cities of today. As the cave-dweller secured food for his family, so this solitary bee, not much larger than a mosquito, stores food sufficient for the needs of its babies in a tiny cavern which it makes in the cliff. Man's evolution has given us canning factories for the storage of our food; the evolution of the bee has given it the hive, and the comb with its golden honey. But the cliff-dwelling bee has no thousands of willing workers to assist it in its arduous labours. With the coming of spring and the blooming of the tea-trees the little female bee seeks out the nectar from the flowers. Well does the bee repay the tea-trees for the supplies of nectar and pollen filched from the blossoms, for it is this bee that performs the valuable service of fertilizing the seeds of the tea-trees by carrying the fertilizing pollen from one flower to the other. Thus the male nucleus from the pollen grain reaches the egg-cell in the ovule within the ovary of the flower.

Often have I watched beneath my microscope the wonder of fertilization of the plant egg-cell by the pollen. Beneath the microscope, by a delicate operation on the flower, the unfertilized egg-cell is removed and placed on a glass slide coated with a sugary solution. This is a female cell, and alone must wither and die. But now, gather a pinch of the powdery golden dust from the stamens of the flower and, selecting beneath the lens one of the minute specks of pollen, place it in the sugary solution some distance from the female cell. The spark of life carried within the pollen grain is male—a male seeking its mate. The female egg-cell also is yearning for fulfilment, and has been busy diffusing throughout the sugary solution a subtle substance, a hormone which calls to the male in the language of the flowers. The pollen grain, that infinitesimal speck of eager male, receives the call, but how can it reach the female? It has no powers of locomotion; it must rely on the bees or other insects to carry it, or a vagrant breeze to waft it to the stigma, the threshold of the dwelling place of the female cells. But the female calls, and the male responds. From out the delicate, jewel-like form of the pollen grain a tiny tube commences to grow. Out it reaches towards the egg-cell; the distance is immense, but, encouraged by the increasing strength of the emanation from the egg-cell it is approaching, it continues steadily onwards. Surely the chasm which separates them is too great, yet the tube does not cease its growth until, in some species, it has reached a length of nearly one thousand times the diameter of the tiny pollen grain from which it originated! The tube reaches the egg-cell, and down the fairy-like pipe line the eager male nucleus joins with the egg-cell in building perhaps some insignificant little weed, perhaps a plant lovely in its adornment of fragrant blossoms, a stately forest giant, or a tea-tree where the tiny native bee sups.

As the little female bee sips from the tea-tree blossoms, the male bee flies swiftly from flower to flower seeking his mate. Here, amidst the sweetness of the flowers, the lovers meet.

But the brief honeymoon is soon over, and she must now fill her short life with arduous endeavour. As her eggs ripen within her she commences to dig into the sandstone cliff. Her strong little jaws bite into the stone, tearing the grains apart. As the debris collects she rakes it away with her feet with all the energy of a fox-terrier at a rabbit burrow. Down and down she digs into the cliff, gathering the debris into pellets, which she carries up out of the shaft and tosses aside before returning to her labours below. Night and day this digging goes on, with only the briefest of visits to the tea-trees for a sip of nectar. Strengthened by her brief meals she continues her work until she has drilled down into the cliff for about fifteen inches—truly a colossal task for such a tiny insect! At the bottom of this completed shaft she now bites out a small cave, about the size of a grain of wheat, at a right angle to the shaft. This cave is to be the nursery for her baby, and she covers the walls of it with silk drapes made from a fluid which she paints on with her tongue. When completed, the little cave gleams like silver.

Now begins a steady journeying backwards and forwards between the tea-tree blossoms and the nursery. Each time the bee returns to the shaft she is heavily laden with pollen and nectar. It was thus that the first lessons of gather and store were instilled into the ancestors of the modern honey-bee. Load after load is brought into the cave, and the pollen and nectar are mixed and kneaded together until she has made a small brown pudding. It grows slowly, for she is such a tiny mite that she cannot carry much on each journey. But she makes up for her lack of size by her ceaseless energy. Her wings become frayed with hard usage, but the ripening egg within her drives her on. At last the gathering of the nectar and pollen and the mixing of the pudding is done, and the little mother lays a pearly egg on the pudding. By now she is weary and worn with her ceaseless drudgery, but there is much yet to be done before she can be sure that the baby she has provided for so well will be safe. With a last look around the nursery she leaves. She will never see the baby for whom she has worked so hard. Wearily she climbs up the shaft to where, about an inch from the top, she builds a platform of sand grains cemented together. Upon this she stands while she commences to build a roof above her head which will completely seal the shaft. Slowly—so slowly—the work progresses, for her strength is fast waning. Although weary and feeble she uses her last scrap of strength to seal the shaft above her head. Now nothing can harm her baby. Her life ebbs slowly away—she sinks to rest at last—in death. The tiny chamber is now her tomb. The tea-tree blossoms fall from the trees, laying a white shroud upon the cliff above her head. No longer do the bees mate amongst the flowers; their short life is over. But beneath the ground the seeds of life in the many little nurseries have quickened.

The egg has now hatched, and from it has come a white grub that commences to feed upon the pudding of nectar and pollen that the little dead mother had prepared for her baby. The last of the food being eaten, the grub rests, and then falls into a sleep that lasts for three hundred and thirty days.

Winter has come to the land above the sleeping baby bee, the cold winds howl and the rains beat down on the earth; but, safe and sheltered within its stone nursery, the baby sleeps on. As it sleeps, a miraculous change is slowly taking place; it still gleams a pearly white, but no longer is it a grub. A miracle of nature is working here beneath the ground, for legs appear, eyes colour, and the slender antennae have grown. The delicate wings have also been fashioned and are folded across the breast. Still the creature sleeps on, while slowly the changes take place. From pearly white the body now takes on the hues of the adult insect; the baby is now an adult bee.

The Demon in the Pit

Above ground the call of spring brings forth the flowers, the tea-trees are abloom. Deep in their earthen cradles the young bees sense the call of the opened blossoms. Our little bee stirs—its legs quiver—its wings flutter—it is awake. Answering the call of spring, it makes its way up the shaft to the world above. But the plug with which the mother had sealed the shaft bars the way. The strong young jaws bite into the stone, the grains are torn apart, and the legs kick the debris free. Soon the first stone barrier is torn down. But now—confronting it—is the dead body of the mother. It is impossible for the bee to know that this is all that remains of its mother, and yet it shrinks back from her dead body. But there is no other way out; to live it must tear apart the body of its own mother. Though aquiver with its desire for freedom, it still hesitates, until with a quick rush the mother's body is torn to pieces and kicked down into the shaft below. With feverish energy the bee tears down the final barrier of sandstone at the entrance and bursts out into the spring sunshine. A moment or two to rest in the sun, then its wings lift it into the air.

It is away to meet its mate amidst the flowers of the tea-trees.

CHAPTER 6

MOTION PICTURES UNDER THE SEA

WE had caravanned thousands of miles through the outback, and sent thousands of feet of film to the southern laboratories for processing. Another wet season was approaching, and every day the thermometer rose well over the century mark. Once the rains began, wherever the caravan happened to be there we would have to stay through the dreary days of leaden skies and steaming earth. There would be no pleasure in each day, brushing green mould from our boots and camera bags. No photography would be possible, and the days would be spent drying out desiccators for the microscope and camera lenses, and moodily watching the sky for a possible break in the constant rains.

Much better to make for a coastal township while the country was still passable, and to set up camp on one of the islands of the Great Barrier Reef. There we should have cool sea breezes and bathing, and since it is during the period shortly before the wet season that the trade-winds cease their steady push and the flat calms are ushered in, there would be an opportunity to put the movie cameras to work beneath the sea.

A few days later we climbed up from the plains, and from the top of the mountain range looked down on the Grand Canal of Australia, the long stretch of sea between the coast of Queensland and the mainland islands within the Great Barrier Reef.

A few hours later the caravan was stored in a barn and, fresh from a luxurious bath in the hotel, we sat drinking cold beer while we made out lists of supplies for the local shops to send down to the boat we had chartered to take us to the reef.

We sailed over an unbelievably blue sea, watching fish with gauzy quivering fins flash from the bows of the boat to skim like birds above the waves, then splash back into the sea a quarter of a mile away. The tops of coconut palms reared their feathery heads above the horizon, soon to be underlined by a snow-white strip, the soft sand of a coral island. The vivid blue of the sea now changed to a lovely translucent green. As we approached the island this green sea was broken by brown and purple patches beneath the surface. The white foam streaming from the bows slid back into the sea as the engines were slowed down. Those brown and purple patches meant coral reefs, and for all their wonder and beauty coral reefs have ripped the bottom from many a stout ship. One of the crew made his way aloft to the cross-trees on the front mast, from where he could plainly see the reefs ahead. The man at the helm watched him intently as the look-out signalled by arm movements the course to take. Dead ahead loomed a great purple patch. The left arm of the look-out man signalled to swing to port. Over went the helm, and the boat swung slowly away from the menace ahead. The right arm now signalled, and the purple patch was left astern. On we went, cautiously threading our way through the labyrinth of reefs until more than two fathoms beneath us we could see, through the sparklingly clear water, masses of alcyonarian corals spreading their great leathery bulk across the floor of the lagoon. With a rattle, down went the anchor, the engine slowed—stopped—and the boat rode in the lee of an island on the Great Barrier Reef of Australia, the greatest coral formation in the world. The reef extends for more than 1200 miles, and is punctuated with scores of tropic isles which need no romantic glamour of fiction to enhance their charm. Many of these islands are surrounded by coral reefs where wonders of sea life flourish in such profusion that, while one never becomes blasé, the feeling of astonishment is perhaps blunted, and one is apt to accept the almost miraculous as the commonplace.

In these tropic waters one finds a happy combination for undersea photography: the water is extremely clear, with the sun shining down in tropic brilliance, and, most happily, it is just this combination that also encourages the prolific growth of coral reefs, with the accompanying flora and fauna.

Making motion pictures in such locations is not so simple as in man's natural environment, dry land. The problems to be solved are many, and there is always a spice of danger to give an added interest. To work successfully beneath the sea nothing must be left to chance. Evolution has developed man as a land animal, and his body has not been designed to bear the enormous pressures to which undersea inhabitants are accustomed. Man is able to stay beneath the sea only if he carries his environment with him. Many people think that the air is pumped down to the diver merely for breathing. This is not so: the air must fulfil two functions—supply oxygen to his lungs, and also surround his body with a cushion, for that is what the air in a diving-suit becomes—a cushion against the relentless pressure of the sea. If by accident this cushion of air is lost, the diver dies a terrible death, for the enormous weight of the sea presses in upon his body with a fearful force, a force that can smash the bones and mash the human tissues to a pulp. Accidents have occurred when a diver has been unable to retain this cushion of air, with the result that his whole body has been rammed into his helmet as an unrecognizable mass of flesh and broken bones. Unless care is taken, diving is always a risky business.

The base camp for our undersea work was a tiny coral island only a few feet above high-water mark. It was chosen because of the clarity of the water surrounding it. The sea near the mainland is never very clear, for the rains and rivers are continually carrying silt down into the ocean, which makes the sea murky and quite unsuitable for undersea photography.

The lugger taking us to our location for the day's work leaves the island about 8.30 a.m. and threads its way cautiously through the reefs to where the sea sparkles clear and blue beyond. It would be useless to start work earlier in the day, for the light dictates the hours of work in undersea photography. The world above may be bathed in brilliant sunshine, but there can still be a partial twilight beneath the sea. This is caused by the angle at which the sun's rays strike the surface. In the early part of the day, or the later part of the afternoon, the sun is nearer the horizon, and the rays, striking a calm ocean at an oblique angle, are partially reflected from the surface; thus the ideal photographic hours are from 9 a.m. to 3 p.m., for then the sun is more overhead and the more vertical rays penetrate deep beneath the surface. If a light breeze keeps the sea dimpled with ripples it no longer presents a flat mirror-like reflecting surface, and thus the ripples present innumerable facets towards the sun, allowing more penetration. Under such circumstances, the light is sometimes satisfactory both earlier in the day and later. Strangely enough, on occasional days without any bright sunlight the conditions can be at their best. This happens on a day when the whole sky is an even white canopy of cloud, for then the light is striking into the sea from all angles, giving a soft yet brilliant light without any harsh shadows.

A glass-bottomed boat is towed behind the lugger, and as we sail along I peer down through the glass. It is like looking through a window into a fairy-tale world lit by a pale blue light. The water is so startlingly clear that ten fathoms beneath one can see the clean sandy bottom, with seashells scattered here and there. In these tropic seas many of them are huge and boldly marked in brilliant colours. Fish of all shapes and sizes glide in ghostly silence through this undersea world. A coral reef drifts into view, and since it appears a likely spot for photography I signal to the captain of the lugger to drop anchor.

Before getting into the diving-suit I put on heavy woollen underpants, a thick woollen sweater, and long woollen stockings. But the purpose of this heavy clothing is not to keep the diver warm: it is often stiflingly hot in the diving-suit under the sea, and the air pump is sometimes packed with ice to cool the air supply. The heavy woollens soak up the perspiration, but they also have another important function: that thick pad of woollens is part of the cushion to defeat the pressure of the sea. Without it the heavy canvas suit, where it touched the body, would soon rub the skin off. A woollen cap is pulled on to the head almost to the eyebrows to soak up the sweat that would otherwise run down into the eyes. Once the metal helmet is on, it is impossible to wipe any perspiration away, and an itchy nose, or worse still, a sneeze, becomes a most uncomfortable experience when in a diving-suit.

So much excess weight is needed to make the diver sink that I have seen men scarcely able to rise to their feet when properly accoutred—let alone walk across the deck and climb over the rail and down the ladder. Despite the weight of the heavy rubberized suit, thick metal corselet, and metal helmet, two lead weights of forty pounds each are fastened to the corselet, one on the breast and one on the back, and boots with lead soles that weigh twenty-five pounds each are necessary too, before the displacement caused by the air imprisoned within the suit can be overcome. And yet, once the diver is below, all sense of weight is lost. In fact, if the valve in the helmet that allows the stale air to escape were closed, the suit would gradually blow up like a balloon, and the diver would float to the surface.

Everything being in order, I clump clumsily across the deck, over the rail, down the ladder, and into the sea. The attendant on deck steadily pays out the lifeline and hose as I descend. The valve at the side of the helmet is gradually opened, allowing the surplus air to hiss out. Letting go the last rungs of the ladder, I sink slowly down through the sea.

Unless one has actually been beneath the sea on a coral reef it is impossible to imagine the unearthly and mysterious beauty of the underwater world. A few yards away everything appears almost as sharp and distinct as if in air; but beyond that distance comes a queer and almost sudden change. The distance from one place to another is hard to calculate, for beyond a small radius things become mysteriously aloof. It is as if they existed in some other dimension, in a world lit with a weird blue light that fades into the distance in a soft curtain of an all-pervading, darker blue.

As I sink down, the pressure increases, but a slight turn of the valve in the helmet holds back the escaping air, and the compressor above quickly forces down that all-important cushion of compressed air, holding back the relentless pressure of the sea. Now the lead soles of my boots touch a huge boulder of coral, and I slide down the side of it, bouncing grotesquely for a moment, and land on the sand, which swirls up like a little cloud of dust round my boots.

As I walk forward a shoal of fish suddenly appears where I would have sworn there was only clear water. These fish have a trick that causes them to become almost invisible, and must be of great use to them as a protection from predaceous fish. They do not swim in the water as fish are usually seen swimming—horizontally; these fish swim vertically, with their snouts pointing to the sand beneath them and their tails to the sky. As I take another step forward they again do their disappearing act, but this time I am close enough to see what actually happens. The whole shoal, just as if controlled by one brain, turns edge on towards me, and now looks like pale, thin, lines. They are a broad, flat fish, but exceedingly thin, and most aptly named razor-fish.

It seems strange that while the razor-fish seem so anxious to hide themselves, most of the shoals of fish swimming round me and darting in and out among the coral seem anxious to attract attention by flaunting their charms before my eyes, for they are as boldly marked and brilliantly coloured as butterflies. However, this gaudiness of marking and coloration is also a form of camouflage, for as I watch there is a sudden weaving here and there of darting fish, and in a flash the scene has lost much of its beauty. The shoals of brilliantly coloured little fish have disappeared amongst the coral as a big fish swims into the scene. Closer observation shows that these bold stripes and brilliant colours actually assist in hiding them, for, like the tiger's stripes that merge so perfectly into the light and shadow of the grasses, the bold markings of many of these fish blend into the patchwork design of the coral reef, with its colourful corals and masses of multi-coloured seaweeds. The little fish seem to be very confident that, if pursued, they can always reach the safety of the coral, for hardly has the big intruder swum majestically from the scene before they come out again and dart about in the open water. They seem to have no fear of the diver in their midst, only curiosity, for they unconcernedly swim about me and even peer inquisitively through the glass in my helmet. One solemn little fish stops in front of me and speculatively eyes the bubbles that are streaming up from the helmet. He is built in such a peculiar fashion that it is difficult to know which is tail and which is head; there is an eye, and what also looks like a mouth at each end! I cautiously reach out a hand, but he dashes off in quite the opposite direction to that which I had expected.

This is a good location for an underwater scene, and I signal for the camera in its watertight case, and the massive undersea tripod to be lowered to me. Although very heavy above water, when under water they weigh about the same as an ordinary movie camera does on land.

I doubt if it is possible to describe the wonder of such a scene. The background of living coral reef has a beauty all its own. The colours of the coral, while not gaudy, are lovely in the mingling of many soft colours: they are like trees, shrubs, and flowers exquisitely sculptured in coloured stone. But the beauty of the tropical fish is startling. Like glittering enamels in their metallic colouring they dash and dart about in search of food. Everything merges into a blur of colour that weaves and changes, reminding one of changing patterns seen through an out-of-focus kaleidoscope. Most people picture these tropical fish as being somewhat the size of the goldfish in the home aquarium, but many of these brilliant beauties are large and weigh several pounds. Even an octopus shows what it can do in the way of decoration. As it comes sliding over the coral, it changes colour more rapidly than a chameleon. When resting on yellow coral, it changes colour to match its surroundings and, gliding forward towards a bed of purple coral, it is silhouetted for a moment before changing to a definite purple shade. It is a queer effect, and the colour change takes place very rapidly. It looks as if the octopus were blushing, perhaps at its bad reputation, which is unearned, for contrary to the many fanciful tales about its savagery it is inoffensive to man and only anxious to get out of his way.

At one time I thought that a shark would be the most dangerous creature one could meet when working beneath the sea. The first time I encountered one of the man-eating species, I was walking along a ledge of coral. A shadow passed over me. I thought nothing of it and continued on my way. When I came to the end of the ledge I stepped off it and dropped a few feet down on to a clear patch of sand. Again the shadow came, but much closer this time. Looking up, I saw a big shark eyeing me intently. It stayed motionless for a few seconds, then suddenly nosed down towards me. Instinctively I groped for the knife at my belt, but then remembered an old trick. Pointing one hand towards the oncoming shark, I slipped a finger of the other hand inside the rubber cuff, and pulled it sharply outwards. Immediately a silvery jet of bubbles rushed from the cuff towards the shark, which slewed to one side. I followed its movements with my outstretched arm, from whence the bubbles streamed as if from a hose. The shark hesitated, then with a powerful flick of its tail and an eel-like twist of its big body, swung around and darted away.

If that had been a giant groper the story might have been different. I have seen many huge gropers, but have never had an encounter with one of these monsters. Divers who have not been so fortunate have told me that the groper's method of attack is much more danger-ous than that of a shark. From what I have observed, a shark circles warily around for some time, and seems to be doubtful about attacking; but, like the tiger that lurks in hiding waiting for its prey to come within leaping distance, the groper lurks among the rocks and coral caves from where it makes a short, deadly rush before the diver even knows of its proximity. The giant groper is really a huge perch weighing several hundredweight, and grows to six or seven feet in length. It is extremely powerful and of great girth. The gape of the jaw is large enough to engulf the head and shoulders of an average-sized man. Since any moving object attracts the groper, it is liable to snap at the diver's air hose and may bite it through, in which case, even if the monster does not attack, the diver is in great danger unless he can immediately signal to be drawn up. This is not the end of his peril, for if he has been working at some depth, he must be drawn to the surface very slowly to allow the nitrogen, which has been forced into the blood stream by the pressure, to escape gradually; otherwise the blood will bubble in his veins like a newly opened bottle of champagne, and that means death, or diver's paralysis. Apart from the hiss of the air coming into the helmet, it is a quiet world beneath the sea. But once I was startled to hear a human voice suddenly break the silence. Another diver was working with me and things were not going too well. The swirl of the current was making it difficult to place some apparatus in position. As we struggled to get things fastened down, our helmets bumped together and I heard my companion swearing vigorously. The tone of his voice was peculiarly metallic and muffled, rather like the sound of a badly tuned radio, but we found it possible, with a certain amount of difficulty, to carry on a conversation as long as our helmets were touching. That diver is now dead, and he died as he once told me he would wish to die, whilst at work under the sea.

I have had one narrow escape myself, and it is not the kind of death I would choose. On that particular day the sea was too rough for photographic work, so while waiting for better weather I set out on a search for a new location for underwater scenes. As we sailed along, I watched the undersea panorama through the water glass. Rising from the depths was the top of a hill, with lovely grottoes going back into the hillside. It may seem peculiar to be talking about hills under the sea, but it is similar to dry land—there are hills and valleys and plains, the only difference being that they are surrounded by water, not air.

This was just the type of scene I was looking for, so the lugger was sailed into position above the hill, and anchors put down fore and aft. I got into the suit and went overboard expecting to land on top of the hill, which woud have been only about forty feet under the surface; but the anchors had not taken firm hold, and no one had noticed that the boat was slowly drifting.

We had had a change of crew on deck, and the man who was acting as tender had not had a great deal of experience at this work. As I sank down, he paid out the lifeline too rapidly, and I passed the top of the hill where I should have landed. It was some distance away, and I realized then that the boat must have drifted, and I was going down—down into the blue depths. I signalled on the lifeline to "cease lowering" but it was being paid out so rapidly that it was slack in my hand, and before I could prevent it, the slack had twisted round my leg. The pressure of the sea was increasing at an alarming rate, and I closed the air escape valve in my helmet. Still I sank down, all the time trying to draw in the slack of the lifeline so that the attendant on deck could feel my signals. But now a more serious situation arose, for as the pressure increased, the air came more and more slowly into the helmet. When going down so deep the engine that drives the air compressor should have been speeded up to overcome the pressure of the sea, but on deck they had no idea that I was down so far, believing I had landed safely on the hilltop. I knew now that death was very close, for as I sank lower and lower the grip of the sea was becoming terrific. The diving suit was pressing in against my legs as if it was made of iron, and there was no comforting hiss of air coming from above. I could see the sea floor coming up to meet me, and wondered if I should reach it alive. If it had been a few feet lower the last breath of air would have been squeezed out of my lungs by the dead pressing weight of the sea. Coils of the lifeline were now lying all about me on the sand; I could see them faintly through a red, swirling mist. I managed to grope my way towards them and feverishly pulled in the slack. At last the lifeline came taut and I signalled desperately "More air! More air!" It could only have been a short time before they realized on deck what had happened and

The author deep down on the sea-floor hands the camera to an assistant
who takes it to the surface to be reloaded with film.

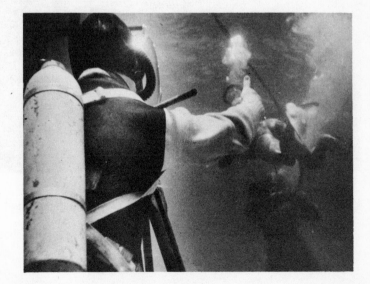

"Thumbs up" is the signal
that the camera is going
into action to shoot the
next scene.

The author films a scene in *King of the Coral Sea*
of the pearl diver at work in the depths.

Noel Monkman, director of undersea photography for South International
Films, with film actors Charles Tingwell and Chips Rafferty.

It is impossible to use a tripod when fish must be followed as they swim,
so the camera is supported on wings.

raced the engine up, but it seemed like hours to me. Mingled with a feeling of intense rage that such a thing should have happened, was a feeling of utter helplessness. One cannot walk out of the danger, cannot call for assistance; in fact there is absolutely nothing to be done except leave everything to those on deck. The feeling of isolation and loneliness is appalling. I felt that at any moment my eyes would be pushed out of their sockets, and the beat of my heart labouring under the strain thudded in my ears like a bass drum. I think that thudding beat prevented me from hearing the first faint hiss of the air as the pressure was built up on deck. When I did realize that the air was slowly coming down, I was nearly unconscious, but despite the searing pain in my chest, I still desperately hung on to the air in my lungs knowing that if I let it go I would never be able to draw another breath against the crushing weight of the sea. Vaguely I realized that I must signal to be drawn up but, as in a nightmare, I seemed unable to move quickly. It was as if in slow motion that I weakly gave the signal to be drawn up, and then must have gone out to it for a moment or two. The next thing I remember was rising rapidly through the sea with my suit ballooning out. I had been too far gone to adjust the valve in the helmet as the air pressure built up inside the suit. Just in time I glimpsed the keel of the lugger above me, and with a tremendous effort forced my arm to the helmet and opened the valve again, thus cutting down my excess buoyancy. It was not soon enough to stop the too rapid ascent, but it helped, for although I struck the keel of the boat heavily enough to dent the helmet, I was not stunned and started to work my way along the bottom of the boat towards the ladder, thinking to myself that I must look like a gigantic, clumsy fly walking along a ceiling. At last I grasped the underwater rungs of the ladder leading to the deck, and laboriously dragged myself from rung to rung upwards. Then my helmet broke the surface, and that was as far as I was able to climb, for as I started to leave the water the weight of the diving suit increased, and I was too weak to climb any farther. One of my native boys realized why I was making no further progress and dived overboard. Getting on the ladder under the water, he lifted my lead-weighted boots upward from rung to rung, and soon I rolled over the rail and on to the deck. When the diving suit was taken off I found that where the diving suit had gripped the flesh my body was a mass of oozing blood bruises, an ear-drum was ruptured, and my chest muscles ached for a week afterwards.

It was fortunate for me that the trouble had occurred so soon after I went below. If I had been working for some time at that depth and had then been blown up to the surface so rapidly with an expanded suit, the nitrogen dissolved in my blood stream would have expanded and bubbled like frothing champagne, and that could only have meant at the best—death, at the worst—diver's paralysis.

The pressing invitation to take up permanent residence in the locker of Mr Davy Jones resulted in a violent attack of claustrophobia each time the diving helmet was lowered over my head. There was an almost uncontrollable impulse to push the helmet away, and it was difficult to remain still and conceal my feeling of utter panic while the helmet was being screwed down. To add to this, I had lost all confidence in the ability of the deck crew to carry out their duties without mistakes. Each new day I awoke with a feeling of crushing depression. Would this be the day I was to be squeezed to death by the ruthless sea? All the joy I had experienced in the world beneath the sea was lost for ever. Working under the sea had become for me just a dreadful nightmare.

CHAPTER 7

THE FREEDOM OF THE SEA

A DAY arrived when I sent the boat to the mainland to pick up some gear I had ordered from overseas. The boat returned with a tin trunk from which I unpacked two steel bottles of compressed air attached to which was a circular mechanism like an alarm clock without a dial. This was an ingenious valve which should throttle the two thousand pounds air pressure in the steel bottles and allow the air to pass like a gentle zephyr through short rubber tubes to a rubber mouth piece. A few straps of fabric webbing permitted this apparatus to be fastened on my back where it was as comfortable as a knapsack. The trunk also contained a close-fitting rubber helmet like a bathing cap with a glass face-plate, a belt with a few pounds of lead, and rubber flippers that made my feet look like those of a giant frog. That was all! No coils of air hose and lifeline—no stiff, rubberized canvas suit, with its heavy metal corselet and helmet—no heavy lead boots nor lead weights on back and chest. Surely this could not be the whole apparatus, they must have forgotten to pack the rest of it. I stood hesitantly on the rail of the boat gripping the rubber mouthpiece between my teeth and through the glass in the rubber helmet looked down into the clear blue water. This could not be true. It required cumbersome gear for man to enter the inhospitable world of the underseas—that is if he wished to return alive. There was but one way to prove it. I drew a deep breath and stepped off the rail. Down I shot feet first into the warm sea, grimly holding on to that deep breath from the world above me. The rush of the water along my body slowed—then stopped. This must be how Mahomet felt as he lay in his coffin suspended between Heaven and Earth. Was I tangled in some rope left carelessly trailing overboard? I knew I could stay underwater for two minutes with the air I had brought with me in my lungs, but in that two minutes I must get free and back to the surface. Quickly I twisted around. I was not tangled—there were no ropes trailing in the sea around me. Instinctively I kicked vigorously. I shot forward.

57

Those rubber flippers gave a giant thrust, and—I had no weight!—a most extraordinary sensation. If I stopped swimming I neither ascended nor descended in the water—just stayed put. Now for the crucial test. I breathed some of the air out of my lungs, and heard the quick ripple of the bubbles rushing upward, then, expecting the worst, I drew a cautious breath inwards. Gently, cool sweet air filled my lungs, I breathed in and out. It was just as if I was breathing in the world above me. Beating the water with the rubber flippers on my feet I moved steadily forward, then with a feeling close to rapture I glided smoothly down to visit the fishes amidst the coral reefs. The fascinating undersea world was mine again more fully than ever before. Never again, when I sat down on the box while the cumbrous metal helmet was lowered over my head to be screwed down on to the diving suit, need I sit surreptitiously on my hands to prevent them, in a frenzied panic, thrusting aside the hated helmet in which I would be entombed until helpers unscrewed the metal nuts and bolts to set me free. No hose, no lifeline would hold me captive to the deck. And never again would I be dependent upon the crew on deck doing the right thing at the right time. If in the future I was unfortunate enough to have to remain permanently with Davy Jones, I would at least have the satisfaction of being the one personally responsible for accepting the invitation. That tin trunk had contained, not only an aqualung, but the freedom of the sea. At last I had returned, and now belonged, to the sea as did the ancient ancestors from whom all mankind has evolved.

It seems strange that we humans should have lost so completely all ability to be at home in the sea from birth. Each and every one of us begin life, as did our ancient ancestors tens of millions of years ago, as a single-celled organism living in a sea. Each fertilized human egg cell lives for months completely immersed in the salt sea of the amniotic fluid of the mother's womb. Here we race through our embryonic past, evolving from the protozoa (the single-celled) to the metazoa (many-celled), reliving those times when we lived in the ancient seas of the world's beginning. For a brief period we sport the gill clefts of the fishes, then long discarded characteristics of the amphibians are hurriedly built by our busy cells, only to be torn down again to be rebuilt into the more highly evolved structure of the organism called man. Only nine months to travel millions of years; yet we can read the stations as we flash past to the destination where we are born as squalling landlubbers drawing air into our lungs to be carried through our arteries by the red blood corpuscles floating in the salty remnants of the ancient seas which aeons ago were locked away in the swirling currents of our closed blood stream.

Why then, since the sea is in our blood, should all these centuries have been necessary for man to invent a satisfactory method of returning even for a short visit to his ancestral home, the sea?

Insects and spiders have been using self-contained diving-suits for many thousands of years. The water beetles lift their domed wing covers to take in a supply of air beneath them, then dive into the water to search for their living prey in the underwater world. Here they courageously attack creatures often much larger than themselves. Down in the depths they fight their desperate battles, relying upon the air stored beneath their wing cases to enable them to breathe during the struggle. Even the modern invention of the submarine schnorkel is ancient history to the larvae of the water beetles, which each possess a slender tube that is protruded and pushed above the surface of the water when their air supply needs renewing.

And what of the diving bell of the water spider? Unlike man, this spider has not forgotten how to live in the underwater world. The spider uses the hairs growing on its body to trap and hold an air supply when it dives down into the ponds. Here, in the cool depths, it spins a diving bell of cobwebs. Returning to the surface it enmeshes a fresh supply of air. Diving down again it scrapes the air bubbles from its body, allowing this air to be trapped in the cobweb. Trip after trip is made to the surface until all the water is forced out of the cobweb dome which now gleams in the pond like a tiny, silver bell. The spider now takes up residence in its underwater home. Soon a web is spun around the submerged dwelling, and the spider becomes a busy fisherman, harvesting a bountiful living from the small water-life ensnared in the silken net. If this spider is a female she will not long remain alone. A male spider, wearing his aqualung of air bubbles, is sure to sight her villa and spy on her until satisfied that she is a lass he could love. Busily he builds another tiny diving bell alongside her residence, with the walls in actual contact—semi-detached, as it were.

Driven by consuming love for the girl next door, the male bites through the adjoining walls and enters her home. Does she run screaming out the front door? No. Almost certainly she makes a quick rush at her impetuous suitor—and eats him. There may be many silken tents vacant and forlorn around the citadel of the proud lady before love brings gentleness and understanding. But passion wanes. The honeymoon is over. She eats her husband to gather strength for her confinement. Soon, a loving mother, she moves serenely about her duties in her crowded nursery beneath the water.

But this is in fresh water. Are there, then, air-breathing inhabitants of the sea? The largest animal in the world is an air-breathing land animal that has returned to the sea, the whale. It is only one of many —turtles, seals and walrus, are amongst the others. These are large and powerful creatures that can contend with angry seas; but do any insects live in the sea? My aqualung introduced me to an insect living in the tropic sea sixty miles from the north-east coast of Australia. Here, in the wet season, devastating cyclones rage, yet here lived these tiny insects. The new-found joy of using the aqualung had coaxed me into the sea on a day when stormy skies made undersea photography impossible. I had been swimming through majestic canyons, and exploring coral caves along an isolated reef, when I realized that I had been submerged for an hour and my air supply was running low. When using an aqualung it is much easier to swim underwater than it is to plod ahead on the surface where the apparatus is a definite hindrance. I decided it would be easier to surface, then signal to the boat crew to come and pick me up. Pulling the release that set free an extra five minutes emergency air supply, I swam back towards the exit of the cave. It was like approaching a magnificent painting. Perfectly framed by the stalactite and stalagmite coral formations of the cave entrance was the lovely translucent blue background of the sea, with a big shoal of yellowtails swimming past in stately formation. Ducking under a swaying festoon of stinging hydroids that fringed the mouth of the cave like delicate curtains of lace, I sped upwards past a mountainside clothed in a patchwork quilt of rainbow-hued corals. Reaching the surface I signalled the lookout man on deck to come and get me, then swam towards the top of the coral mountain which the falling tide had uncovered for a few inches. As I started to clamber up on the coral I saw a sudden movement. A number of small creatures scuttled across the exposed coral into the sea, and continued running down the mountainside under the water to disappear beneath a stony ledge some distance below. In the fleeting glimpse they had looked like insects, not sea creatures, but surely that was impossible away out here in the open sea. Unstrapping the empty air bottles, I placed them on top of the coral as a marker for the boat crew, and dived down after the mysterious creatures. I slid beneath the ledge and looked up. There they were rapidly scrambling along the underside of the ledge towards a number of deep and roomy crevices. With my face-plate only a few inches from them I could see every detail. Two—four—six legs, all other observable characteristics added up. Yes, no doubt about it —they were insects! But how could they live and breathe beneath the sea? Then I solved the mystery. Many of the crevices under the ledge were actually diving bells. At low tide the ledge was above water; as the tide rose again the air was trapped in these crevices making homes for these hardy seafarers. Here, while storms shrieked and raged above, they could safely shelter in their secluded, air-locked caverns. When low tides left the coral exposed, they wandered about the mountain-top looking for food or basking in the tropical sunshine. With my air bottles refilled I dived down again and lay under the ledge watching these queer little insects going about their daily lives. Always they clung to the coral reef and never attempted to swim—a very sensible habit. If they trusted themselves to the water, the swirling currents would almost certainly prevent them returning to the safety of the reef, and they would be swept into the open sea where they would soon become exhausted and drown. I watched them stroll down to the shore line of their undersea villages, where they would gaze fixedly into the sea beneath them. Suddenly they would make a quick grab into the water and haul out some almost invisible prey which they would devour with quite dainty table manners.

The ledge had many well-populated villages, and as these creatures were strange to me I captured two and sent them for classification to an entomologist of the Australian Museum. In return I received a letter asking for more specimens, preserved in tubes of spirits, as these were insects of a species new to science. By the time that letter reached me

I was exploring another reef hundreds of miles away from the courageous little inhabitants of that outpost of insect empire. I admit I was happy to be unable to fulfil the further requirements of the entomologist. After all, they were now properly recorded in the census of world population, and since their ancestors and my ancestors down through the ages had managed successfully to adapt themselves to all the tremendous changes in world conditions, we held certain rights in common. The first of these rights was to live; the second, to enjoy the freedom of the sea.

CHAPTER 8

ARCHITECTS AND ARTISANS OF THE CORAL REEFS

ALTHOUGH in the mass a coral reef appears a brownish-purple, at close quarters this effect is entirely lost, for then one is surrounded by a mosaic of colour. No hard brilliance of colouring dazzles the eyes; each colony seems to merge into the other in a soft mingling of pastel shades. But colourful it is, with every colour of the rainbow. And what diversity of form is here! Jutting out from the edge of the reef are widespread fans, two or three feet across. Some formations are like great bunches of chrysanthemums, others like the antlers of a stag, and this one like a candelbra with blue candles that seem to be burning beneath the sea, for each blue candle has a flame-like tip of yellow. One might imagine that one was in a field on land, for surely they are mushrooms growing over there; but pick one up—it, too, is hard, stony coral. Even a gruesome replica of the human brain is here in this fantastic garden. But not all the growths in this coral garden are hard and stony. Alcyonarians, or soft corals, flourish luxuriantly, but are more subdued in colour—soft greys, yellows, delicate lavenders, browns, and greens. These soft corals are in large formations, many of them yards across, and they spread their great leathery bulk in all directions. But they have a beauty of form that gives a piquancy to the scene, while their softer colourings only throw into greater prominence the brighter colours of the hard corals and the warmly tinted seaweeds. Although the alcyonarians have no skeleton of hard stone like the madreporarian corals, they have the power of extracting carbonate of lime from the sea; but they build it into dainty spicules which, while they strengthen the formation, still leave it pliable enough to sway gracefully with the surge of the currents.

The loveliness and the strength of the coral reefs have been built by creatures many of which are so minute that a microscope is necessary to see them. Even in these enlightened days, one still reads in books and magazines of "the coral insect which builds the coral reefs"; but no matter how powerful a lens is used to examine the coral, it will

63

never show you a coral insect, for no such creature exists, nor has the coral polyp the slightest resemblance to an insect. Even the most casual observer knows that an insect has legs and can move from place to place; the coral polyp has no legs and remains firmly attached to the limy formation with which it surrounds itself. It is the bleached skeleton only that one sees in specimens of coral in museums. This formation should really be called a "corallium", but the common usage of the term "coral" for these structures would perhaps make it confusing if I pedantically insisted upon the more correct nomenclature; therefore such formations shall be called "corals". They are composed of carbonate of lime which the living coral polyps extract from the seawater and use to build these massive structures. These bleached skeletons have the beauty of form of the living corals, but can show us nothing of the glory of colour that is the first thing to hold the eye when one views a coral reef. The rich colouring lies within the tissues of the polyps, and when they die only the white, limy skeleton remains. The colouring of living coral is of little assistance in identification, for one species may vary through a wide range of colourings, and even the shape can be so changed by environment that its classification would puzzle anyone but a specialist in corals: in rough water, a massive formation with heavy, clubbed branches can be of the same species as a fragile coral with fine, branching twigs growing in sheltered waters.

One of the alcyonarian corals, the organ-pipe coral, has not the white skeleton of the madreporarian corals, but has a beautifully constructed skeleton of closely compacted spicules of a rich, red colour. These spicules are built into a series of tubes with supporting braces in regular spacing. In life, each tube is occupied by a coral polyp, but a dead specimen shows nothing but a regular formation of the crimson tubes, with a very definite likeness in miniature to the pipes of an organ. In a living specimen nothing of this skeleton can be seen, for it is hidden by a curtain of bright green polyps, which, unlike many species of coral polyps, are fully extended and protruding from their tubes in the day-time. The majority of coral polyps emerge from their stony homes to feed at night, and in another chapter ("Pastures of the Sea") I shall explain why their food is more plentiful after sunset. If you look closely at any specimen of dead coral you will see that it is a mass of tiny pores. Each of these was once the home of a minute coral polyp, and these wee animals are the architects and artisans of the reefs. By their combined labours they build the great coral barriers that curb the mighty power of the sea. In their dying they give birth to the lovely coral islands, for they leave their skeletons to be ground into coral sands, where sea birds may nest, trees may grow, and man may dwell.

A dead specimen can show us little of the beauty of living coral, and it requires a microscope to reveal the loveliness of the fragile creatures that built it. At first glance it would be excusable to doubt if these were animals, so readily might they be mistaken for flowers. But no flowers behave like coral polyps. They are carnivorous animals that paralyse their prey with poisoned darts, then with their dainty, petal-like tentacles pass the helpless victim to the mouth, which opens in the centre of the flower-like polyp. The common anemones of the rock pools are close relatives of the coral polyp, but the anemone has never learnt the art of building a stony home by extracting calcium carbonate from the sea water.

Like the anemone, the coral polyp has only a single body cavity, which has to serve the purpose of a general body cavity, as well as performing the work of digestion. It is like a sack, with but one opening through which the food enters, and all waste matter is discarded. This coelenteron, or body cavity, also functions to a degree as our lungs do, or the gills of fishes, for, as the sea water flows into the stomach, the tissues of its lining absorb oxygen, as do all other parts of the polyp that are in contact with the sea. But this is not its only method of breathing. Under a high-powered microscope innumerable tiny spherical cells may be seen throughout the living tissues of the polyps. These are not animal cells, but vegetable cells, which attend to their own feeding and reproduction. They are not parasites, nor do they irritate or injure the coral polyp. In fact, the plants and the animals in whose tissues they live are mutually benefited by the association. This mutually satisfactory partnership is not uncommon in nature; there are many instances of its occurrence, not only between plant and animal, but also between animal and animal.

The vegetable cells growing within the tissues of the coral polyp utilize the action of the sun's rays upon the chlorophyll in their cells and the carbon dioxide given off by the coral polyp, and in return supply the polyp with oxygen, which is as necessary to it as the tiny animals it captures for its food. But the partnership goes even farther, for during the day many coral polyps withdraw into their stony homes leaving exposed to the sunlight the very parts of their bodies that are most densely crowded with the plant cells. Thus conditions are most favourable for the plants, which can now use the sun's rays to the full. This not only benefits the plant cells, but ensures a more plentiful supply of oxygen for the coral polyps, for plants give off oxygen when exposed to the rays of the sun.

There is a very remarkable instance of association between an animal, *Convoluta*, and a vegetable cell, *Zoochlorella*, which shows how far this dependence, one upon the other, may go. *Convoluta* is a small worm that makes brilliant green patches on the sand when the tide recedes. The worm, buried beneath the sand when the tide is in, must seize the opportunity of bathing in the sunlight the moment the water leaves the sands, for without the sunlight it would starve to death. In its youth, *Convoluta*, like other flat-worms, fed on small animals, while the green algae, *Zoochlorella*, multiplied within its tissues. The worm then found the starch manufactured by these vegetable cells an adequate source of nutriment, so it no longer sought for animal food, but became a vegetarian; and now it feeds exclusively upon the algae. Within a short time, because of disuse, the digestive organs of the worm atrophy, and the worm is no longer able to feed upon anything but the vegetable cells within its own tissues. Since plant cells must have sunlight for their growth, *Convoluta* is forced to become a gardener, and must devote all the hours of sunlight to tending the garden within its tissues. This is the reason for the emergence of the flat-worm from its burrow in the sand as soon as the water has withdrawn, for now the sun must shine upon the worm and so reach the plant cells which require sunlight to manufacture the starch, which is then eaten by the flat-worm. So far, so good, and during these days it is a happy partnership. But the flat-worm has a habit of begetting its kind (as is the manner of animals), and while it is building a new generation, its appetite increases. Herein lies tragedy, for *Convoluta* makes such serious inroads upon the algae that the plants cannot multiply fast enough to keep up with the demand, and since the worm has lost the ability to eat any other kind of food, it slowly starves. After laying an enormous number of eggs, *Convoluta* dies, having as it were, killed the goose that laid the golden egg.

Like all animals, the coral polyp must at one time have been a baby, but in its baby period it bears no resemblance to the creature that builds and lives in the hard, stony corals. It has a strange sex life. At certain seasons of the year the coral polyps extrude a milky fluid that contains millions of the male elements. These male elements, or spermatozoa, are widely disseminated throughout the water by the action of the ocean currents, and are drawn in through the mouths of other polyps during the process of feeding, for, as I have already stated, the mouth is the only opening into the body cavity. Within the mesenteries of the coral polyps are masses of female cells or eggs. The male sperms make their way to these eggs and fertilize them. The eggs now develop into tiny, pear-shaped organisms covered with fine, vibrating hairs (cilia). These baby corals are called planulae. When they have developed to this stage, the parent polyp ejects them through the mouth. They are tiny creatures, the largest being about one-fifteenth of an inch across, and from some species of coral they are the tiniest of microscopic specks.

With the hairs upon their bodies beating vigorously, they make their way towards the surface of the sea. Here they are carried far and wide by the currents and tides, thus being distributed as are plant seeds by the winds. During this free swimming period, the planula changes in shape. No longer does it look like a pear, for an indentation has developed at the end of it, which keeps pressing inwards until the shape has changed to that of a tiny cup. Its free swimming period is now ended and, if it is fortunate enough to find some suitable place in which to grow, it attaches itself by a cement-like fluid which it secretes. Millions of the planulae are unable to find a suitable situation in which to establish themselves, and they perish. Those that have been more fortunate immediately set to work to extract from the water the calcium carbonate with which to build their homes. Seen through the microscope the young coral is now of exquisite and fragile beauty, like a tiny, crystal goblet from which the little builder, now a coral polyp, extrudes its petal-like tentacles and commences to feed.

But not for long is the tiny coral alone. Within a short period, fission, or the dividing of one into two, takes place, and now two little goblets stand where there was but one. Soon fission takes place again, and now there are four, and so the process goes on, like the story of the ten little nigger boys in reverse.

The coral colony is now firmly established, and it may grow until there are hundreds of thousands of polyps in one great coral formation, every member of the colony having come into existence by splitting off from its fellows. The vegetable cells (*zooxanthellae*) are also thickly distributed throughout the colony, for when the tiny planula left the mouth of its parent to establish the new colony, it carried within its tissues a share of these plant cells, and before fission takes place, each new polyp receives its share of the plants, which grow apace within their host.

There are many varieties of coral, with different structures and habits peculiar to the species, but to enlarge upon these details is not the purpose of this book. Broadly speaking, the life histories of all the varieties do not differ in any main essential from the one I have already given. Some have more or less tentacles than those of another species; some kill their prey with poisonous, barbed darts; others have no poisoned darts but possess innumerable hairs on their tentacles which vigorously lash the water and create currents which stream towards the mouth of the polyp, carrying the tiny creatures upon which they prey to be engulfed in the central opening or mouth. There is a great deal yet to be done in the study of corals; many secrets are yet to be discovered, and many wonders await revelation.

It is many years since I made my first motion picture of the life of the coral. I had blithely set out on the production of this film without realizing the obstacles that would confront me. Because of certain desirable characteristics in the species I chose to film, I overlooked a most serious problem. I knew that the coral polyps would only emerge at night, but this had not worried me as I had a very efficient lighting system available. However, when I commenced to use the microscope with the motion picture camera, the extremely intense arc light, which I was forced to use in order to obtain well-exposed pictures, affected the coral polyps so much that they withdrew, and would not emerge again until the lights were put out. Coral polyps have no eyes, and yet this species was sensitive to light, although it would not appear to be the light that brought about an awareness in the creature of when was day and when was night. During my experiments I had a small coral colony living in a glass tank in my darkroom, for I also wished to study the effect of darkness upon those vegetable cells that grew within the living coral. Naturally, there was no change between day and night in the darkroom, and yet, ruled by some strange inner rhythm, the coral polyps withdrew into the coral while it was daylight outside, and emerged when the sun had sunk to rest. There appeared to have been nothing that could have made the creatures aware of when the sun rose or night fell. In filming them, however, the brilliant light made them withdraw at night, and it took six months of ceaseless experimenting before I devised a method to overcome this difficulty and obtained the first motion picture ever taken of living coral polyps emerging from the coral and feeding upon the microscopic life of the sea.

CHAPTER 9

CURIOSITIES OF A CORAL REEF

Fascinating as the study of coral may be, it is but a small part of the wonder of the reef. When an ambitious coral colony has grown too high, the low tides leave it uncovered. This causes its death, for it cannot live if exposed to the air for too long a period. But though it is dead, there is much life beneath it. What a scurrying takes place as we lift it, for many reef creatures make their homes beneath the dead coral.

Moving agitatedly about are several creatures resembling in shape the Australian army badge with its radiating rays, but in this case the rays, which extend from the creature, are the flexible tentacles of a shell-fish. It is *Lima*, a swimming bivalve. When the crimson tentacles are partially withdrawn within the shell, the creature looks much like ordinary bivalve but with a wide crimson edge, which is the tentacles neatly coiled up but still too bulky to be drawn completely within the shelter of the shell. The *Lima* shares with the scallop, and some other bivalves, the unusual distinction of being one of the few shell-fish that can swim, and it is no clumsy tiro. Slowly it parts the two shells and spreads out its beautiful crimson tentacles, then quickly snaps the two shells together. This sudden closing of the shells drives the *Lima* speedily through the water, trailing the tentacles behind it like the tail of a comet. Soon it finds shelter again beneath the adjacent coral.

But the departure of the *Lima* is almost unnoticed, for there are so many other creatures claiming our attention. The largest of these are sausage-shaped objects of various sizes and colours. The Malays call them trepang—a romantic-sounding word, it rings like an Eastern gong; but there is nothing romantic about the creatures themselves. We call them bêche-de-mer or sea-slugs, and in their lethargic habits they are indeed most sluggish animals. This green one looks like a prickly cucumber, and that long one like a black snake—it even has a red belly like the black snake of our bush, but it is quite harmless.

Alcyonarian corals spreading their great leathery bulk
across the floor of the lagoon. (Underwater photo.)

The beauty of a coral garden.

Even a gruesome replica of the human brain is here in this fantastic garden.
(From the film *Coral and Its Creatures.*)

Our base camp was on a tiny coral island.

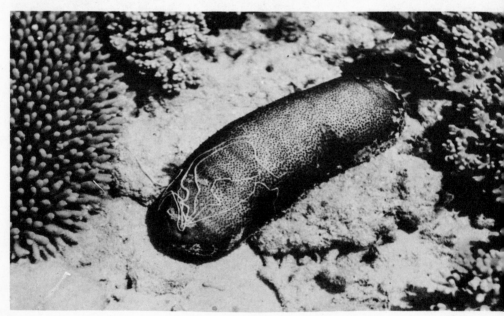

Bêche-de-mer. From a small opening in the hinder end, out streams a mass of milky white threads. (Underwater photo from the film *Ocean Oddities*.)

Press that stout, orange-coloured one firmly with your finger, and from a small opening in the hinder end out streams a mass of milky white threads that look like spaghetti. But do not touch those threads, for they are the stickiest things imaginable, and it is an exasperating job to free your fingers from their unpleasant, clinging grip. If any other creature attacks it, the bêche-de-mer has no chance of escape, for its movements are slow, and it has no teeth with which to defend itself. Those trailing white threads are its intestines, and its only means of defence; the bêche-de-mer relies upon them to entangle and discourage an enemy. It can draw the threads back into its body again if they are not damaged, but this is an unimportant detail to the creature, for it can discard its intestines and grow a new set to replace them.

Lying on the reef is another snake-like creature about five feet in length. It is *Synapta*, a relative of the bêche-de-mer—quite a handsome creature, with its alternating rings of greenish-brown and putty colour. At its head is a ring of tentacles, each shaped like the frond of a fern, which are in continuous action. The creature uses these to pick up sand, which is then conveyed to the mouth in the centre of the ring of tentacles. Here the sand is removed from the tentacles with a movement like that of a child licking jam from its fingers. The bêche-de-mer method of feeding could be likened to putting food through a sieve, for the greater part of the material swallowed contains no nourishment; but as it passes through the long alimentary tract all organic matter is extracted, and the residue of sand, pieces of shell and broken coral pass out of the body. If you lift the *Synapta* up, it is like a thin sausage-skin full of water. The water running to the dangling ends of the creature proves too heavy for the strength of the skin, which soon tears, and the *Synapta* commences to break up. But you have not caused its death, for the portion that bears the tentacles is the head, and it will grow a new body. When handled, the *Synapta* clings to the fingers as if its skin were sticky. This apparent stickiness is caused by minute, calcareous spicules embedded in its skin, and so tiny are they that a microscope must be used to examine them. Under the lens we discover that the *Synapta* discovered the anchor long before man, for distributed throughout its skin are beautiful plates and myriads of tiny, glass-like anchors. It is the points of these anchors protruding through the skin that cling to the fingers. The *Synapta* uses these tiny spicules as anchors, and their myriad points gripping the sand prevent the currents from rolling it helplessly about on the reef.

Before the war there was a considerable industry in bêche-de-mer fishing along the Barrier Reef. Native luggers scoured the reef for these creatures, which were then gutted, and smoked in trays above fires of red mangrove wood. After this treatment the bêche-de-mer looks most unappetizing. The main purchasers of the dried bêche-de-mer are the Chinese, who use them to make a soup which they consider has remarkable aphrodisiac qualities. For my part, if the lady was so lacking in charm that it became necessary to assimilate soup made from what looks like shrivelled up old boots, I should never be a Casanova.

It seems difficult to believe that the slug-like bêche-de-mer are relatives of the starfish and the sea urchins, but so it is. When the creatures are dissected and studied, the anatomical similarity and the relationship become obvious. The coral reefs abound in an astonishing variety of starfishes, from very tiny ones to others more than a foot across. The starfish most often seen is a brilliant blue one that shows no outward signs of life, and even when picked up remains stiff and rigid as if petrified; but beneath nearly every piece of dead coral is a squirming mass like a bunch of hairy, wriggling worms. Each of these frantically writhing creatures is a brittle-star which, unlike the blue starfish, moves with considerable activity by lateral movements of their long, flexible arms—which they discard with great readiness. If you capture one it immediately starts to break off pieces of the writhing arms; and if it is irritated enough, soon nothing will be left but the central disc and a scattered array of severed but still wriggling arms. The central disc, however, has the power of re-growing a complete new set. Indeed, even with most careful handling it is quite a feat to secure one of these well named brittle starfish all in one piece. One of the best methods is to lower a jar cautiously under the water and carefully manoeuvre the creature into the jar. But your problem is not yet solved, for as soon as it realizes it is trapped it will commence to throw away its arms. But carry with you a strong solution of magnesium sulphate in sea water and immediately add some to the water in your jar. This acts as an anaesthetic, and the brittle-star quietens down and soon dozes off. Many fragile sea creatures may be captured by this method; but here is a strange thing: magnesium sulphate is ordinary Epsom-salt, and upon humans its action is hardly that associated with anaesthesia.

There is no need to resort to similar methods when capturing the pincushion starfish, which possesses no arms at all. This species grows very large and often weighs several pounds. It bears quite an absurd resemblance to the fat pincushions that adorned the chest of drawers in grandma's day; it even possesses little coloured protuberances on its skin like the old-fashioned, glass-headed pins. The majority of starfishes move slowly over the reef, for, although they have hundreds of feet, using them to walk on is quite a complicated business. Turn the creature on its back and you will see its feet, rows of them, waving in all directions, each one like a small, flexible tube with a flat disc at the end. To use its feet the starfish extends them by pumping them full of water; the foot then lengthens, and the starfish takes hold with the disc at the end of the foot, which acts as a sucker. Now the water is withdrawn and the foot contracts, moving the creature forward a fraction of an inch at a time. A starfish in a hurry moves about two or three inches in a minute. It is a stayer rather than a sprinter, and this is well illustrated when it dines upon an oyster. Slowly it creeps forward until the oyster is completely covered by the body and arms of the starfish. Upon its approach, the oyster has, by contracting its powerful adductor muscle, snapped the two valves of its shell tightly together. The starfish would appear to be merely resting on the oyster, and gives no sign of the grim battle that is in progress. The tube feet have a firm grasp of the two oyster shells, and the starfish is exerting all its strength to pull the shells apart; but the adductor muscle of the oyster is much too powerful, and it easily keeps it shells tightly closed. Minute after minute the battle goes on, and as the oyster wearies the starfish keeps up its unrelenting pull. The tired oyster eventually relaxes, and inexorably the starfish drags the shells apart. Then the starfish performs a most amazing feat. Instead of conveying the oyster to its stomach, it conveys its stomach to the oyster! Out of the mouth of the starfish comes its stomach, which is pushed inside the shell and over the oyster; the oyster is devoured inside its own shell. The meal digested, the starfish withdraws its stomach back into its body and slowly moves on, leaving two empty shells of mother-of-pearl agleam in the sunshine.

The starfishes of the Barrier Reef would often seem to prefer to make a meal of their relatives, the spiny sea-urchins, rather than the succulent oyster. The sea-urchin is often called the sea hedgehog because of the hundreds of sharp spines, like a veritable wall of spears, projecting from the globular case that houses the soft tissues of the animal. The starfish, disregarding the wounds that may ensue, wraps its arms around the spiny creature and, exerting a steady pressure, snaps the spines off. Now having broken down the outer line of defence, it gathers the sea-urchin more closely to it. The sea-urchin now brings into play its inner line of defence. These are smaller spines, but instead of being spears, they are sharp and powerful nippers that bite deep into the tube feet of the starfish. But as I have said, the starfish is a stayer, and retains its harsh grip on its intended meal. Soon the nippers break off under the steady pressure and remain embedded in the tube feet of the starfish. Now, bereft of all armaments, the sea urchin is vanquished, and its cousin, the starfish, devours the piquant flesh of its helpless relative.

It may not be so difficult to realize the relationship between the starfishes and the sea-urchins if you imagine the arms of an ordinary starfish bent backwards until the tips touch, then imagine those arms becoming joined along their sides. You have now imagined what nature has evolved in the sea-urchin. But it has gone farther and has covered the body with sharp, movable spines. It has, however, retained the tube feet of the starfish, and if you look carefully between the spines you will see hundreds of these tube feet in action. Sea-urchins are well represented on the reef, and one species, the needle-spined sea-urchin, a handsome creature although clothed in sombre black, may be found congregated in great numbers in a patch of reef only a few yards in extent. I once counted ninety in one small pool. The spines upon their bodies were about a foot in length, and swimming in and out among these spines were shoals of gaily coloured little fish. Whenever a large fish approached, the little fellows would dart for shelter to the spines of the sea-urchin from where they would look out belligerently with a "come and get us" expression. The tiny fish shelter-

ing among the spines of the sea-urchin is but one example of the need
so many creatures of the reef have for protection. The reef is a battle-
field of ceaseless warfare, with a slogan of "eat, or be eaten", and
strange indeed are the methods adopted by the weaker ones to ensure
their continued existence.

There is an amazing instance of one creature seeking shelter
within the body of another: a thin, eel-like fish, four or five inches long,
called *Fierasfer*, which, when alarmed, darts for shelter by passing
through the anus of one of the bêche-de-mer, and hides in its hind
gut. It is a most startling experience to see one of these fish poke its
head out of the bêche-de-mer and look round to see if the coast is
clear before emerging again.

Another little fish called *Actinicola percula*, of a bright orange with
white bands outlined in black, would have but a slender hope of
survival if it were not for its association with the giant sea anemone.
The two or three inches of brilliantly coloured little fish makes it
very conspicuous. This being so, it clings closer than a brother to the
anemone and, if alarmed, will dash in amongst the tentacles of the
anemone, or even, if hard pressed, go into the anemone's mouth and
shelter in its stomach!

The most remarkable feature of the association between this little
fish and the anemone is the complete immunity of the fish to the
powerful stings with which the tentacles of the anemone are loaded.
These stings are similar to those possessed by the corals. Studded
along the tentacles are rows of nematocysts, microscopic cells like tiny
bladders distended with poison. Coiled within each poison-cell is a
fine, barbed hair. These bladders have a small spike like a trigger
projecting from the surface of the cell, and should some creature touch
this trigger, the poison-cell immediately ruptures, and out dart the
long hairs that plunge into the body of the victim, carrying the poison
into the wounds. Should the creature so poisoned be small enough to
be eaten by the anemone, it is passed to the mouth in the centre
of the tentacles; any larger creature retreats with a skinful of stings
to teach it caution. And yet there are several species of gaily coloured
fish to which the anemone extends special privileges, allowing them to
nestle unscathed amongst its batteries of stings. The usual food of the
anemones is small crabs and shrimps, but there is also a small crab,

75

and a shrimp, that share with the little fish the wonderful protection afforded by the anemone. Most likely it is not so much the goodwill of the anemone that ensures their freedom from being stung to death, as their own natural immunity from the poison.

While we were making motion pictures on Nor' West Island in the Capricorn Group on the Great Barrier Reef, Kitty made friends with two little fish that lived in an anemone a short distance out on the reef from our laboratory. They were pretty little fellows of a dark reddish-brown, with bright orange fins and tail, and a bold stripe of vivid turquoise blue across the head. This blue stripe on the head looked like a bandage, and with the lugubrious expression given by their sadly downturned mouths, one could imagine that they had tied their heads up to ease a raging toothache. They were pugnacious little fish, and would leave the shelter of the anemone to chase away any smaller fish that came near their chosen home. Kitty named them Mutt and Jeff, and after a few days they grew so tame that they would nibble at food held in her hand. But a sudden wriggle of her fingers would send them scurrying back for shelter to the protecting folds of the anemone.

The anemone, despite its batteries of stings, is not always immune from attack, for there is a creature that not only eats the anemone, but actually uses the stings for its own protection. It is a nudibranch or sea-slug and, unlike the bêche-de-mer which is also often called a sea-slug, this creature has none of the characteristics one usually associates with slugs. Many of them are gorgeously coloured—one species being orange, crimson, and snowy white, with what appears to be a golden lotus growing from its back. The name, nudibranch, means naked breathing organs; for the animal carries them outside its body, protruding from its back. These branchiae are often very ornate, being branched or pinnate processes having the appearance of exotic flowers or gay rosettes of filmy ribbons. A nudibranch usually creeps slowly over the sand; but if you touch it it leaves the sand and swims. And what swimming! I know of no movement in nature more gracious, and never tire of the joy of witnessing it again. The nudibranch is oval and flat, the body tapering away to a diaphanous fringe which in its graceful undulations reminds one of the pleasing skirt dances so popular in our theatres years ago. There is something almost ethereal in the effortless ease and smoothness of the creature's progress.

There are many species of nudibranch, some of them most striking in their brilliant, contrasting colours, and yet it is some of these beautiful animals that savagely make a meal of the flower-like anemones, apparently finding an added relish in the bladders of poison that stud the tentacles of this creature. Having extracted the nutriment from its meal, the nudibranch stores the poisoned darts in special organs that project from its body, and now uses these stings for its own protection.

There are many creatures on the reef with a Borgia complex, for poison is quite a common means of protection. Sea-snakes are there, much like land snakes in appearance, except that their tails are flattened for swimming. Like many land snakes, they too possess fangs loaded with poison, which is often more venomous than that of their land-lubber cousins. But you need not fear them, for they are not aggressive, and dart away at your approach.

Of course it is asking for trouble to grope about with the hands under any coral or rock on the reef: you may encounter a snake that may bite if alarmed; but it is more likely that a fish will be the creature to poison you. Be cautious when turning over stones, and be sure that you are grasping a stone, and not a stone-fish, for this is the most dreaded of all the creatures on the reef. I have often pointed one out to newcomers to be met with a blank stare and, "What fish? Where?"

The stone-fish is a master of camouflage, and only a practised eye can pick it out as it lies amongst the dead coral. With a stick you can push it clear of the coral on to the sand. It does not attempt to swim away, but obstinately persists in its impersonation of a stone. Here is no shining mail of scales, but a wrinkled, warty skin of a dingy grey, with blotches of dirty green, as if here was a body that putrefied while it still lived. It seldom grows to more than nine or ten inches in length, but its deadliness cannot be calculated in inches. Its small grey eyes peer coldly out from deep pits in its head, and coarsely textured fins like daubs of mud project from its body and lie flat on the sand. It is difficult to believe that such an unwholesome-looking thing can be a living fish. But the stone-fish has every reason to be complacent about its appearance, for its likeness to a weed-encrusted stone ensures the capture of its meals. It lies motionless awaiting the approach of small, unsuspecting fish or unwary crabs, then suddenly the undershot jaw moves, disclosing a gaping mouth with a sickly, pale-green lining, and with a quick snap, the victim is engulfed; and again the stone-fish is motionless as a rock. A snake relies upon only two poison fangs, but the stone-fish can erect upon its back a row of thirteen sharply pointed spines, which have grooves in their sides by which a most virulent poison, from internal glands, is injected if the spines penetrate the flesh.

A sea creature attacking a stone-fish is immediately pierced and poisoned, resulting in almost certain death. Human beings who have been unfortunate enough to place their foot on what appeared to be only a stone have paid for their carelessness with weeks of agonizing pain and long months of illness, and some have carried a deformed foot for life. But they have been the comparatively fortunate ones, for others who have stepped upon a stone-fish have stepped out of this life, so potent is the poison manufactured by this creature which science has named *Synanceja horrida*. The poison affects the nerves, and the only relief that can be given to sufferers is to inject narcotics until the agonizing pain has to some extent abated.

The coastal aborigines of tropical Australia know well the danger of the stone-fish, and make certain that the children of the tribe will realize this danger. They have a special corroboree that depicts the men of the tribe spearing on the reef. One of the tribesmen stands upon a model of a stone-fish manufactured from beeswax. Shrieking in well assumed agony, the native falls to the ground where he rolls backwards and forwards in apparent paroxysms of pain. So the youngsters learn to tread warily on the reef, and their eyes are amazingly quick to detect this hated fish.

Poisonous stings need not necessarily be associated with ugliness. In the quiet pools on the reef may often be found a relative of the stone-fish, the butterfly cod, a fish of flamboyant beauty. Like the stone-fish, it does not grow to any great size, twelve inches being a very large specimen and, again like the stone-fish, it is a slow swimmer. But its stately progress through the water gives it greater opportunity for display. Its dorsal and pectoral fins look like gorgeous, widespread fans. It is these spreading fins that have given it the name of butterfly cod. Body and fins are striped with bands of scarlet on a cream ground. The spreading ventral fins are a deep velvety purple spotted with white. The large tail is of a transparent, gauzy texture patterned with black spots. The spines upon its back carry waving colourful pennants. But it is as well to remember that Mother Nature often gives us a kindly warning, and bright colours on many creatures can be regarded as danger signals; so let the butterfly cod go on its stately way untouched. If those long spines with their trailing draperies prick your hands, you will experience a sharp, burning pain that will remind you for several hours to let well alone. It is not surprising that a fish of such distinctive beauty should have been widely noticed, but unfortunately observers in different localities have given it names to describe the characteristics that most impressed them in regard to it. So it has been variously named the butterfly cod, the fire fish, the lion fish and the scorpion fish: an example of the necessity for scientific nomenclature. To prevent confusion science has only one name for this fish—*Pterois volitans*.

Another interesting fish one is likely to encounter on the reef is the toado fish. It has a large head and a greenish-coloured body that looks much like that of any other fish until it is alarmed or attacked; then it uses a quaint method of protection. It is a slow swimmer and has little chance of escape by swimming away, so it just stays where it is, and commences to pump itself full of water until it is blown up into an oval shape as firm and hard as a football. Standing out from its rotund, white belly are innumerable spines. Any fish that thought the toado would make an easy meal would leave in disgust, for it could not even get a decent bite at it in this inflated condition. Perhaps is it just as well, for the flesh of several species of toadoes is poisonous.

Do not imagine that many of the creatures that live on the reef are seeking to bring about your death; you are quite safe if you use ordinary commonsense. I have been wandering on reefs for many years and have never been injured by any of the reef creatures. But a word of warning: until you are familiar with the reef and its inhabitants, as the Scots say, "Gae canny."

There would seem to be no danger whatever in collecting pretty shells, and yet, unless you know what you are about, you are in grave

79

danger of being stung by a snail that lives in just the kind of shell you would be anxious to pick up, elated to have such a pretty specimen to add to your collection. When you think of sea-snails do not think that they invariably possess shells like those of the land snail. There is one similarity between the snail shells of sea and land—they are both spirally wound, but to prevent confusion forget your land snails when you wander on the reef. The snail shells of the sea are of every variety of shape, colour and design, some so small that a microscope must be used to see their beauty, and all sizes in between up to those large enough to require both hands to hold them comfortably.

The shell that is dangerous is one of the cone shells, of which there are many species, bearing upon their outer surfaces intricate designs with rich colourings. The animals that build these shells can extrude through the mouth a hollow spine that is connected to a reservoir in the body where a potent poison is manufactured and stored. In several instances it has caused the death of people who have handled this shell carelessly, and at the best, should one be stung, severe pain and temporary paralysis can result. In spite of this, do not think harshly of the creatures of the reef: the majority are quite harmless, and these poison-bearers are, after all, not attacking you, but merely defending themselves.

So, shell collectors, be wise in time, and learn to recognize your *Conus* at a glance.

CHAPTER 10

MORE QUEER CREATURES

W E have already discovered that a sea-slug can be a thing of
beauty, so it is not surprising to find that a sea-worm can be
a joy for ever. Scattered liberally amongst the coral are small patches
of bright colour. Look closely at one of these and you will see a structure of great delicacy and beauty. Most of them are not very large,
about half an inch in diameter, and have the appearance of a bizarre
little flower growing on the coral. But if you attempt to pluck one—like
a flash, it is gone! Even the shadow of your approaching hand is
enough to cause its disappearance. Where the apparent flower once
bloomed is now seen to be the end of a tube with a smooth lid
which, fitting snugly, seals the tube against any intruder. That pretty
little flower was the corallate gills of a serpulid, rejoicing in the
scientific description "tubiculous polychaete annelid", which in plain
English means a tube-inhabiting, many-bristled, worm. The little
flower is actually the worm's prettily coloured foliaceous tentacles.
These are protruded from the tube with the dual purpose of obtaining food and oxygen from the sea water. On the tentacles, or perhaps
they should be more correctly called gill filaments, are innumerable
fine hairs which by their synchronous lashing create a circulation of
the surrounding water. As the water passes over these tentacles, oxygen
is absorbed from the water which is kept moving by the cilia towards
the mouth of the worm, situated in the centre of the crown of
tentacles. These currents carry to the waiting mouth the minute
organisms upon which the worm feeds.

When making a motion picture of this worm, I wished to show
that, despite the crown with which it was adorned, its body was just
that of a plain, ordinary worm; but since they never leave their tube
homes, and were so quick at slamming the door in my face, for some
time I was at a loss to know how to obtain a photograph of the complete animal. Eventually I succeeded by placing the serpulid, still
in its tube, in a small tank of sea water. I waited for its lovely crown

to appear, then slowly, drop by drop, added a very dilute solution of cocaine to the sea water. It had to be done very carefully, for had the worm realized what was happening it would have snapped back into its tube and closed the door. But since I was not a doctor with a full waiting-room, there was no need to hurry the job, and after a few hours of slowly administering the anaesthetic, my serpulid dozed off. Gently I took hold of it with a pair of forceps, and drew the sleeping worm from its tube. What a shock it was to see that pale, rather repulsive body, after previously seeing nothing but its lovely ornamental crown. There are many varieties of serpulids, and between them they exhaust the spectrum in their use of colours.

Beautiful as are the ornamental crowns of the Serpulidae, and varied as the colours may be, at least they remain that colour. But this is not the case with another creature which smoothly glides into our ken. It looks like the blade of a broad spear. As we watch it swimming along it suddenly seems to de-materialize. Peering more closely at the spot where it was last seen, we see that the creature is still there, but how different it now looks! When first sighted it was a rich chocolate brown, now it is but a ghost of its former self, a misty, translucent grey, shot with pale pink and blue. It is a squid, which, like its relative the octopus, has this chameleon-like power of colour change. But the chameleon is a mere amateur compared with the squid, and has to have time to adjust itself to a new colour. Not so the squid—in the blink of an eye it changes colour. A most ingenious mechanism enables it to perform this feat. Throughout its skin are tiny pigment cells, each of which contains one particular colour. Attached to the corners of these cells are small muscles which, by relaxing or expanding, can increase or decrease the size of the pigment cells. For instance, if the squid changes to a brown colour, the muscles that are attached to the corners of the brown pigment cells contract, thus stretching these cells until each cell nearly touches its brown neighbour, giving an all-pervading brown hue to the squid. It may be simpler to picture what actually happens by imagining a child with a fair skin liberally be-sprinkled with freckles. Now imagine each of those freckles stretched until it touched its neighbour. No longer would the child have a white skin powdered with freckles; it would have an unmottled skin, as if evenly sun-tanned. The octopus also has this power of changing colour, and employs the same method.

The ability to change colour so rapidly could make the squid a master of camouflage; yet frequently it appears rather to desire to be conspicuous. Often, without any apparent reason, it blushes from one colour to the other through its entire repertoire of colour changes, not merging into the colour of its surroundings but standing out in contrast against them. It may be that the squid uses its colour changes for a more subtle purpose than that of mere camouflage, for I have often seen one that had assumed a light, indefinite hue that made it semi-invisible suddenly change to a dark, bold colouring at the very moment when it darted in amongst a shoal of small fish. The sudden appearance of the squid in their midst created utter panic amongst its prey, which, in an attempt to escape, darted this way and that in a most bewildered fashion. The octopus-like arms of the squid struck unerringly at the frightened fish, and seized and conveyed them to the parrot-like beak, which killed them with one vicious bite.

If the squid itself is attacked by some large fish, it has three trump cards to play. First it uses its sudden colour changes to bewilder its pursuer. If this fails, it creates a smoke-screen by suddenly ejecting a cloud of sepia into the water. If the pursuer still persists and dashes through the smoke-screen, the squid is almost certain to have eluded its enemy, for at the very moment it ejects the sepia cloud, it turns at a sharp right-angle to its previous line of travel, leaving the pursuer to blunder on through the clouded water while it flees at incredible speed in quite a different direction. One of our most modern war developments has been that of the jet-propelled aeroplane, but this is old news to the squid, for it has been using jet-propulsion for thousands of years. The stomach and other vital organs of the squid are contained in a muscular bag. It draws the sea water into this bag, then, by a powerful contraction, expels the water with tremendous force through a flexible spout—its syphon, which lies where the tentacles join the body. It is the flexibility of this syphon that gives the squid the ability to dash off at a tangent, for it merely swings the syphon into a new position, and the force of the expelled water drives it like a rocket in the opposite direction.

The interstices of the coral afford shelter to innumerable creatures, but one of them is not satisfied with any stray crevice or cranny, and actually forces the coral polyps to build it a home. It is a small crab, commonly called the gall-crab, which in its young days settles down in the angle between two growing stems of branching coral. Because of its presence the coral cannot develop normally, for where the crab rests, the polyps die. But the polyps all around the crab continue building, and eventually the crab is in possession of a snug little cavity inside the growing coral. The crab takes care that a small opening is left to the outside world through which the oxygen-bearing water and the microscopic organisms on which the crab feeds can gain entrance. The crab that causes the coral to build this home is the female, and though she is now in possession of a snug little house its tiny doorway is from one point of view a disadvantage. The male of the species is a much smaller crab and has no difficulty in visiting the female by entering the small aperture through which she gets her food and water. The period of love-making over, he departs. The female crab is so much larger than the male that she can never leave her home, but must live her whole life imprisoned in the cavity in the coral. The baby crabs leave home when even smaller than their father, and the daughters make the same mistake as their mother in designing homes with small doorways.

The lot of womankind may be hard, but consider how hard may be the lot of the male of another species of crab. One day on the reef I captured a male that had been attacked by a parasitic creature named *Sacculina*, which is itself a crustacean and a distant relative of the crab. Beneath the body of the crab was hanging a small sac which was packed with the reproductive elements of the parasite, almost ready to break free and go in search of other crabs to prey on. If this had been a female crab, it would not have outwardly appeared that *Sacculina* had caused her any serious damage, but since it was a male crab, the results were disastrous.

Sacculina bores a hole through the hard shell of the crab and, having reached the tissues, has no further use for its own shell, which it discards before making its way inside the crab's body, where it is eventually transported by the blood stream to the intestines. Here it develops and, like a plant, slowly sends out roots that reach into every part of the crab's body. As *Sacculina* develops within its host, an amazing change takes place in the male crab. By some weird miracle, the structure of the body is altered; he grows broad and matronly in figure; the fine, big claws he used to flourish so pugnaciously become smaller and daintier in appearance. As a crowning disgrace, he may actually discard his masculinity and—lay eggs! In the old days, B.S. (before *Sacculina*) he used to moult regularly and appear in a natty new shell; but now he will never moult again, and must wear his old suit for the rest of his life.

The moulting of crabs is essential for their growth. When they are youngsters and growing rapidly, moulting is very frequent; for the crab grows within its shell, and since the shell is not elastic the growing crab finds the shell a cramped prison from which it is forced to escape. It is quite an uncanny sight to see a crab moulting. The action is reminiscent of one of those double-exposed motion picture scenes where the supposed spirit of an actor sits up, stands, and then walks away, leaving his dead body behind him. The back of the crab's shell splits, and a soft, ghost-like creature slowly draws itself out from the hard shell, then scurries away, leaving its old shell lying empty on the sand. The newly emerged crab must find a secluded refuge, for it is now a soft creature, and not able to cope with the rough and tumble of reef life. Within a few days, however, it has grown a hard, new shell, and is once more able to take its place among its fellows.

During the time between leaving the old shell and growing the new, the crab has been, as it were, out of its corsets, and its soft body has been able to expand, so the new shell is no longer cramping, but comfortably fits its extra bulk. As the crab gets older moulting is required less often, for the creature is then attaining its maximum size.

There is another crab that also has to change its shell as it grows, but it does not grow the shell itself, it simply appropriates one. As we turn over the stones on the reefs, shells of various kinds and sizes scuttle for cover. These scampering shells are invariably univalves, yet they move in a manner and at a speed quite impossible to any univalve. The creatures that inhabit them are called hermit-crabs, surely a most inappropriate name, for they have most unhermit-like habits.

The higher crustaceans belong to two great groups. Science has given the name Macrura to one of these groups, and to the other,

Brachyura. Respectively the meaning of these two names is "long-bellied" and "short-bellied". The sub-order Macrura can be readily recognized in the freshwater crayfish and the lobsters of the sea. Those long bellies are gastronomically appreciated by most of us. The crabs belong to the sub-order Brachyura, and how different is the short belly of the crab from that of the lobster. If you pick up a crab and turn it over, you will see just how insignificant is its hinder body. Tucked close underneath is a flat, inconspicuous tail, in shape not unlike a lobster's, but it would almost escape notice unless you happen to have picked up a female crab which is in "berry", or in other words, clasping a mass of tiny eggs to her body with her small tail.

The hermit-crab's hinder body is not like that of the lobster, with its heavy plates of armour and fan-like tail, nor is it an insignificant, flat thing like that of some other crabs. The hinder body of the hermit-crab is plump and soft, bearing no armour at all. Herein lies the reason for its use of discarded univalve shells, for while it does not possess an Achilles' heel, it does possess an extremely vulnerable and tender behind. So unusual is this soft body that some scientists considered the hermit-crab should be given a group of its own in scientific nomenclature, and suggested that it should be named Anomura, the translation of which is "nameless-bellied".

Well, that seems to dispose of the crab portion of the hermit-crab's name, but why the hermit? It would, I think, be universally agreed that a hermit is one who withdraws from association with his fellows and lives in solitude. But the hermit-crabs are gregarious and seek each other's company. It must be admitted that they seem to forgather either for the purpose of quarrelling, for they are most pugnacious creatures, or, if not following Mars, they fall into the lap of Venus, for they are most ardent lovers. I cannot remember ever having heard of a hermit who delighted in the practice of either love or war!

A further instance of the unhermit-like habits of the hermit-crab is in its association with two other creatures, a worm and a sea anemone. The worm, which is called *Nereis*, is often found living in the same shell as the hermit-crab. *Nereis* is a carnivorous creature, and may be seen swimming in the open pools amongst the coral, and a most savage and voracious hunter this worm is. Do not picture these sea-worms as being similar in appearance to land worms. Many sea-

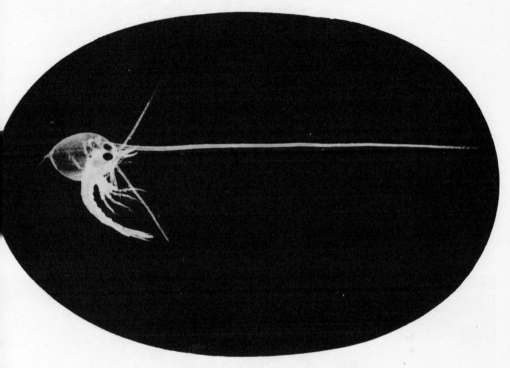

When first discovered, this needle-nosed creature was thought to be a new species of animal. Actually it is the zoea stage that, when about the size of a pin-head, changes into a lobster-like megalopa stage, then changes again into a baby crab.

Not even when its larger opponent pulled the claws from the smaller crab's body would it give in. (Underwater photo from the film *Strange Sea Shells*.)

The victor rammed his own body in on all that was left of his opponent. (Underwater photo from the film *Strange Sea Shells*.)

worms are most active creatures, swimming with graceful undulations of their bodies; others possess rows of rythmically beating feet that propel them rapidly through the water. As *Nereis* swims, no offensive weapons are seen, but when the prey is about to be seized, what a transformation occurs! The head of the worm protrudes, displaying formidable pincer-like jaws, and these hard and powerful mandibles soon rend the unfortunate victim. Having taken up living-quarters with the hermit-crab, *Nereis* becomes something of a home body, for now there is no necessity to scour the pools for food: the hermit-crab carries *Nereis* from one place to another, and when its host feeds, *Nereis* emerges from the shell and joins in the meal.

The partnership between the sea anemone and the hermit-crab, however, is a more satisfactory arrangement for the crab: while the worm merely purloins portions of its partner's meals without making any return, the anemone and the hermit-crab are mutually benefited by their association. The anemone lives attached to the outside of the shell, and is always ready to discharge a broadside of poison darts into any enemy that may attack the hermit-crab. In return for this protection the anemone secures a meal from the scraps that drift about it when the hermit-crab is feeding. The hermit-crab is obviously aware of the advantage of having the artillery of the anemone on the roof-top, for if a change of shell becomes necessary the hermit-crab carefully removes the anemone from the old shell and places it on the roof of its new home.

Apart from eating, loving, and fighting, the main occupation of the hermit-crab is house-hunting, for as it grows the sitting-room in its shell becomes cramped, and so every shell it encounters in its wanderings is looked upon as a potential home. It matters not how worn and dilapidated the shell may be, it is always given a thorough examination with a view to occupation. Perhaps the new shell is too small—perhaps only half the size of the one the hermit-crab already possesses. Even so, it is turned this way and that, claws are inserted in the shell, and perhaps it is even given a try-out as a residence. This movement from one shell to the other must be carefully observed, for it is done so speedily that the details may easily be missed. It would seem that the creature is always aware of the danger of exposing its soft body to attack by a reef inhabitant. To make the change

over the crab carefully places the new shell in position with its opening facing it; it grips the edge of the new shell with its claws, then
in a flash withdraws its body from the old home and slips its tail into
the new. The hermit-crab now attempts to back completely into the
shell until nothing can be seen but its heavily armoured claws barring
the doorway. If the new shell happens to be too small, the crab cannot
back far enough into it, and after a few ineffectual attempts to ram
itself deeper into the shell, it whips back into its previous home.

But while all this has been going on, another hermit-crab in
search of a new home has appeared on the scene. The newcomer
immediately attacks, and our hermit-crab wheels valiantly to meet the
unprovoked attack. With their big claws extended, the combatants
clash together; it is all-in fighting, with no holds barred. Backwards
and forwards rages the battle, as each furiously attempts to pull its
opponent from its shell. Fortunately, apart from the tender hind part,
hermit-crabs are as heavily armoured as any crab. Here is a point to
ponder upon in watching this miniature battle. Many a time I have
attempted to drag a hermit-crab from its shell; it will part with its
limbs (it will later grow new ones), but it will not relinquish its
hold upon the shell. If one exerts too much force, the hermit-crab
will be torn in half rather than allow its tender body to be withdrawn
from the shell. And yet it is obvious that each of the contestants is
attempting to do this very thing to its opponent. For its size, the
hermit-crab is very powerful, and can support nearly thirty times the
weight of its own body by the grip of one claw. We humans, unless
trained athletes, can seldom support more than two-thirds of the
weight of our bodies with the grip of the right hand.) The pull of the
crab on its opponent is nothing as compared to the force a human hand
can exert when attempting to drag a hermit-crab from its shell: no
hermit-crab's strength is sufficient to tear its opponent in half. How
then can either warrior expect to vanquish his foe?

The explanation is that the hermit-crabs use the tactics of "nerve
warfare". Each crab relies upon the fury and bluster of its attack to
bluff its opponent into surrender, and the warrior of faint-heart is
beaten before the fight really begins. Since the whole point of the
attack is to pull the other fellow out, the only token of surrender is
for the loser to loosen the powerful tail grip, and allow the victor

crab to pull him out. A strange thing about these fights is that once the vanquished crab is out of its shell the victor never seems to follow up its advantage by attacking its unarmoured and dangerously exposed opponent. The vanquished hermit-crab scuttles away, but only to the nearest cranny in which it can hide its soft body. The victor never pursues, but centres its whole attention upon the now empty shell. Reaching inside with its big claw, it reconnoitres the roominess of the apartment. Satisfied with this, it then turns the shell about, examining it from all angles. Instinct seems to have gone all astray here, for the shell it already occupies may be a handsome one, and certainly a more suitable size for the proportions of its owner; whereas the shell of the vanquished is perhaps a battered specimen liberally bespattered with limy incrustations and empty worm tubes. However, a change of abode is soon made and, leaving its previous pleasant home behind, the victor departs with its tail firmly tucked into its tumbledown shack. It has hardly left the scene before the loser in the battle scuttles out of the cavity where it has been sheltering and swiftly takes possession of the handsome new house lately vacated by the winner of the fight.

Peering out from this new home, he sights a small hermit-crab wandering across the bottom of the pool. With a sudden rush he is across the sand, but not before the smaller crab has had a chance to withdraw into its shell. He rolls the other shell over and feels inside, but the small crab has withdrawn far back into the shell, and his large claw cannot force its way into the doorway. Straddling the shell he waits. What a bully! Does he wish to forget his late defeat by a victory over this small opponent? This crab is only a third his size, and if he drags it from its shell he will never fit his bulky body into a house so small. But this, dear reader, is love: the dainty little shell holds a female hermit-crab!

As I have said, one of the ruling passions of the hermit-crab is love, and his methods are those of the caveman. Coyly the female peers out from her shell. Immediately he makes a quick grab for her, whereupon she withdraws into her shell beyond his reach. Apparently even amongst crabs it is not ladylike to appear too willing. Impatiently her lover waits outside her doorway, but not for long, for within a minute or two her long antennae emerge, followed by two eyes on the end of their long stalks, and she surveys her lover. Perhaps pleased with his appearance, she emerges a little further, and in a flash he has grabbed one of her hind-legs and hangs on. At first she tries desperately to get back into her shell, but he ignores her vain struggles and strolls off, dragging her after him by the hind-leg. He may be a boorish lover, but at least he attends to the details of the wedding breakfast, for as he strolls along he pauses now and again to scratch up particles of food, which she accepts as they drift her way. After an hour or so of strolling and feeding in this fashion, he would appear to consider that the honeymoon is proceeding rather slowly, for he now turns round, grips her, and with a sudden jerk lifts her almost free of her shell, and they embrace. This embrace ensures another generation of hermit-crabs.

It is a brief love-making, and although the lady now seems willing to accept his attentions, never does he relinquish his grip on her hind-leg, but continues to stroll about, dragging her willynilly with him. Every hour or so he remembers her, but only long enough for another short embrace. Rounding a clump of coral, he is suddenly attacked by another hermit-crab, who, with a furious buffet, sends him rolling back across the sand. His wife has been flung some distance away, but she quickly rights herself, and calmly commences to pick up small particles of food from the sand, daintily transferring these to her mouth as she watches her husband do battle. The issue is not long in doubt, for with a sudden jerk, the newcomer drags her husband from his shell and casts him to the sand. With a desperate rush, he attempts to regain his shell, but another furious blow sends him tumbling. Taking no further notice of him, the newcomer strolls across to the lady, who is placidly feeding. Within a minute or two he has clasped her dainty hind-leg, and as the former husband regains possession of his shell his wife is accepting the attentions of her new lover.

Usually the fights between hermit-crabs are of short duration. Either one or the other speedily decides it has met its match, and lets itself be drawn from its shell, so concluding the duel. But I once filmed a fight between two hermit-crabs that lasted, off and on, for three days. One crab was slightly smaller than the other, but it would not succumb to the usual war of nerves, and clung tenaciously to its shell. Not even when its larger opponent pulled the claws from the smaller crab's body would it give in, and when it had no further weapons with which to carry on the fight, it withdrew deep within its shell. The victor, evidently considering that the honours of war were his, left his shell and rammed his own body in on top of all that was left of the smaller hermit-crab. This is the only instance I have seen of what appeared to be a fight to the death. It would appear that nearly all hermit-crab fights are a matter of bluffing the other fellow out of his shell.

For sheer entertainment, I can recommend a day watching hermit-crabs.

CHAPTER II

THE PASTURES OF THE SEA

L IGHT and shadow, peace and beauty, with the murmur of the sea breeze in the tree-tops, while one wondered if the feathery coconut palms towering so far aloft had tapped the source of all music, and were whispering it down to a sleepy world. Such was the setting for the laboratory on our tiny coral island.

The sea which surrounds this island of emerald beauty appears a place of even quieter serenity as it lies shining like a mirror of sapphire. Fortunate it is for lovers of the sea that its inhabitants are mute. For what a ghastly clamour would arise from that blue world by day and by night: the anguished shrieks of the myriads dying and the harsh triumphal cries of the victors!

Terrible as has been the human warfare on the sea, beneath the sea, and in the air above it, man's sporadic outbursts of killing are dwarfed by the battles for survival that have been waged for countless ages in all the seas of our planet. Much of this bitter struggle goes on unseen, and so tiny are many of the contestants that our unaided eyes can seen nothing of their ceaseless battle. Wherever there is water, there life will cling and thrive, and it would seem that as long as there is life, some must perish that others may survive. Life is indeed the daughter of death. *Ex nihilo nihil fit*—nothing can come out of nothing. Death must make available to Life the building materials of tomorrow. There is ceaseless turmoil in the soil of our fields where minute organisms are living and dying to prepare the way for future crops. And as blood and bone enriches the land, so does it enrich the sea. As in the fields the grass must grow if the cattle are to be fed, so must there be pastures of the sea to feed its thronging animal life.

A great deal of the teeming life of the sea belongs to the plankton. And what is this thing called plankton? To say that it is like the stars in the heavens in its countless millions and its innumerable dimensions might not be very helpful, but it might convey what an enormous field of infinite variety is covered by the word "plankton". As the astronomer gazes through his telescope to make the very distant stars visible, so we must peer through the lens of the microscope to see much of the very tiny life of the plankton. The microscope becomes a window into a world of wonder, a world inhabited by creatures more bizarre and beautiful than any created by writers of fantasy. To describe adequately what one sees beneath the microscope is beyond the average man. In attempting to round out the description one feels that the adjectives obtrude too readily, and this is apt to become monotonous; yet to describe these microscopic organisms without stressing their beauty would be to describe a waterfall without mentioning the water. Unfortunately, not even photographs can convey the intrinsic beauty of this microscopic life. In motion pictures some of their loveliness is captured, for at least we can see the grace of movement well displayed. But little is reproduced of the scintillating lights flashing across the transparent membranes, or the extremely delicate nuances of colour that are too subtle to be registered by any photographic process of today.

To make film stars of these minute specks of life demands the use of one of the most difficult branches of motion picture photography, cinemicrography. To obtain successful results the apparatus must be of high quality, but even then the technique is exacting, and because the actors are no longer in their natural environment, but are confined to a single drop of water, the problem of merely keeping them alive is often extremely difficult to solve. Most of my films of microscopic sea life have depicted the creatures of the tropic waters, and it is amazing with what speed a drop of water can evaporate in a tropical climate unless special precautions are taken to prevent it. Also, the actors breathe the oxygen in the water around them and, small though they are, the oxygen in a single drop of water is soon exhausted. This must be allowed for and extra supplies made available.

The filming of a life history may mean keeping the creatures in the laboratory for many weeks; and they are hungry little mites, so special arrangements must be made to see that there is always a supply of their favourite food on hand. Once all these matters are attended to, the difficulties really begin. The ocean has no sudden variations of temperature, and our actors are not adapted to withstand the sudden rise caused by the heat of the powerful light required to film them through the microscope. To reduce this rise in temperature the infra-red rays are filtered out of the light beam, as also is the dangerously penetrating ultra-violet light. But this alone is insufficient, and the light must be allowed only to flicker on to the creatures. This flickering light is made to synchronize with the movie camera shutter, so the light is on for only the fraction of a second that each picture is being taken. The air in the laboratory is also much hotter than the sea, so the drop of water in which the actors play their parts must be kept cooled to sea temperatures by using a tiny glass tank which is surrounded by a larger metal tank through which water, kept at sea temperature, is continually circulating. When these details are satisfactorily attended to, the plankton behave as if the one drop of water was an ocean, and enact their life stories as if everything was quite normal.

Plankton is a Greek word that means wandering—a very accurate description of the plants and creatures that make up this community of drifting sea life, which is carried for many hundreds of miles by the ocean currents. Many of the creatures of the benthos (dwellers on the sea bottom) and the nekton (active swimmers—this includes the fish) in the baby stages of their lives belong to the plankton. So now we see that in the study of the plankton we are entering a field of vast dimensions: for it not only includes a big majority of the babies of the larger animals and plants of the sea, but is also made up of myriads of animals and plants which, even when full grown, are so minute that it would take several thousands of them placed end to end to measure one scant inch.

This drifting life is found in the seas at any time of the year, but only at certain periods does it reach its maximum of abundance. Life in the sea and life on the land are each subject to the rhythm of the seasons, and as the spring brings forth the spring blossoms to the land so it brings forth an uprush of new plant growth in the sea. There is also a link between the distribution of land plant seeds and the tiny life of the sea, for as the winds transport the plant seeds to new grounds, so the winds also help to create the great ocean currents in which the plankton is carried and distributed. If it were not for the growth of this plant life, there would be no living creatures in the sea.

With spring there comes a tremendous increase in the number of diatoms in the plankton. Diatoms are plants, and so tiny are they that it would need more than a million of them to fill a teaspoon. They are given the name diatom because of a peculiarity in their structure. The word is from the Greek, *dia*, meaning "through", and *temnō*, "I cut", and when closely examined the structure of the diatom is found to be in two pieces like a tiny pill box. If you could lift the lid of this tiny box, you would find a vegetable cell, with all the wonderful characteristics and power of such cells. Within its tiny compass it performs miracles of chemical transmutations, and contains everything necessary for the reproduction of its kind.

These diatoms are of the utmost importance, for they are the pasturage of the sea. Indeed modern research would indicate that all the life in the sea may depend for its existence upon these and other minute plants. Small as they are, they are found in an infinite variety of shapes and sizes. Sculptured upon their surfaces are intricate designs, the lines of which in some species are less than one hundred-thousandth of an inch apart. To see, or in the language of the microscopist, resolve, these lines, is a severe test for the highest powered lenses made for the microscope. The more one studies diatoms, the more interesting they become. Many microscopists have become so absorbed in the study of these minute plants that they have lost interest in all other branches of microscopy. Their fellow microscopists, who have not fallen under the spell of these jewels of nature, whimsically call these enthusiasts "diatomaniacs". I must admit that I, too, was once one of that happy band, and spent many joyous hours searching for new specimens which I would boil in a test tube of nitric acid, from which the diatoms emerge with the contents destroyed but the skeletons unharmed and their structural beauty revealed. Then I would study them under the microscope, trying by more expert use of the instrument to see just a little more of their structure than had yet been seen. A goodly proportion of my earnings in those years went to purchase better and still better lenses to achieve this purpose. I do not regret those years when I suffered from diatomania for, as the practising of scales develops the technique of the musician, so the efforts to resolve the finest markings on the diatoms develop the technique of the microscopist.

The minuteness of the diatom markings is not the only wonderful

thing about them: their silica skeletons are ornamented with symmetrical patterns. Nature is prodigal of beauty in unexpected and
seldom observed places. The Diatomaceae could quite easily give new
inspiration to a poet, and perhaps I may yet live to read an "Ode to a
Diatom".

It is not the appearance of the diatom's structure that is of practical importance, but the fact that they are the primary food supply
of the sea: but for the diatoms and other minute forms of vegetable
life there would be no living creatures in the sea. Innumerable tiny
animals of the plankton eat the diatoms, which are their main food
supply. These planktonic creatures, which are themselves microscopic
in size, are now eaten by slightly larger creatures; these in turn by
larger again; and this chain of eat and be eaten continues until even
the largest of the fishes is fed. One may truthfully say: as the grass is
to the fields, so are the diatoms to the sea.

To secure specimens of these minute plants, together with other
plants and creatures of the plankton, the sea water is strained through
fine silk made into a long, conical net with a test tube fastened at the
end of the silken cone. When the net is towed through the sea, the
water filters out between the fine meshes of the silk, but the plants
and animals are washed down into the test tube. When the net is
drawn up and the test tube examined, the water in it is murky, for
it is clouded with the dust of the sea. That dust is composed of thousands of diatoms and creatures that depend on them for food.

One might be forgiven for doubting that the diatoms as they
appear under the microscope are really plants, for they possess a power
that is not usually attributed to the vegetable kingdom. Some of these
plants move freely about in the water, for they are able to swim. Just
how they perform this feat is a mystery that has caused many heated
debates among microscopists. Because of the stately movements of the
diatoms, the early naturalists classed them as animals. Then the
botanists found in them certain characteristics that belong to the vegetable kingdom, and claimed them for enrolment in their branch of
science. For years the argument raged, but now we know that the
botanists were right: the diatoms contain a substance akin to chlorophyll, the green colouring matter of plants, and, as is the way of plants,
use the radiant energy of the sun and the chlorophyll-like substance

in their cells to convert the phosphates and nitrates in solution in the sea water into a form that nourishes the protoplasm contained in their tiny, box-like skeletons of silica. Only plants can exist on such primary elements.

Diatoms are not confined to the sea; they are a most ubiquitous form of life and may be found in such diverse places as lakes, streams, pools, on the moss by mountain cascades, in the snow of the Arctic regions, in roofing gutters, and even on the top of stale jam!

In long past ages these minute plants have lived their short span near the surface of the ancient seas, and dying, they have sunk in incalculable billions to the sea floor. This ceaseless rain has continued through long centuries, and the tiny skeletons, lying feet thick at the sea bottom, have been compacted for aeons and eventually converted into a kind of stone called diatomaceous earth. If a small piece of this diatomaceous earth is dropped into a tube of boiling nitric acid, soon nothing remains but the lovely silica skeletons. It is many thousands, perhaps millions of years, since the diatoms were living plants, yet their skeletons are as perfect as the day the plants died, and many can be recognized as species that still flourish luxuriantly in the seas of today.

Diatomaceous earth is used as an absorbent in the manufacture of dynamite; and although in this form it may assist in causing death, in another form it does its share in prolonging human life. Filters for bacteriological laboratories are made of this earth, filters so fine that they strain out the extremely minute bacteria, but allow the chemical substances produced by the bacteria to pass through; so these plants of long ago assist man in his inquiries into disease. The peasants inhabiting certain mountain regions in Europe have found a quaint use for these fossil diatoms. In past ages this part of the continent has been beneath the sea, and by slow geological processes the sea-floor has been raised far above the water. In the bad years when famine stalks these mountain areas and grain is scarce, the peasants, when grinding the grain into flour, add to it a quantity of diatomaceous earth taken from their fields. They call this earth bergmehl, or moun-tain flour, for they believe it contains nourishment. Unfortunately for them this is not so, but at least the added bulk of these countless millions of silica skeletons may to some extent mitigate the sufferings of the poor peasants by filling up the crevices in their empty stomachs.

These ancient diatoms have yet other gifts for man. In life they each contained within the cell a minute droplet of oil, which remained within them as the dead diatoms rained down on the sea-floor. Man drills down into the diatomaceous earth to obtain this oil, which is one of the sources of petrol for the machines of today.

In the drifting community of the sea there are other single-cell organisms, some of which at first sight might be mistaken for diatoms. You will notice that I have not said "plants", nor have I said "animals"; I have carefully evaded the issue by referring to them as single-celled organisms. Science calls these organisms peridinians, and they belong to a half-way world, for while they have the usual characteristic of plant life, having chlorophyll stored in their cells, and while they absorb through their cell walls the gases and salts dissolved in the sea water, they also possess a characteristic of animal life: they have a small pit on the surface of the cell wall that functions as a mouth, and through this the organism swallows solid food. No wonder the zoologist and the botanist nearly came to blows when attempting to classify such an organism.

Whether they are animals or plants, the peridinians continue to swim blithely in the ocean, each moving along by the action of two little whips, which by their vigorous lashing of the water propel the organisms along. In some parts of the sea they congregate in such enormous quantities that they colour the water over wide areas in patches of red, green, or blue. Some species even kill the fish in their vicinity, for the organisms, dying in enormous quantities, may putrefy and temporarily poison that area of the sea.

There is yet another group of unicellular plants of the plankton of which there are a great number of species, all possessing within the cell a number of microscopic calcareous plates the details of which are used as a means of establishing the identity of the species. This group is named the coccospheres. Diatoms, peridinians, and the coccospheres are most important groups in the plant life of the plankton, and form the main food-supply for the minute animal life that is so enormously abundant in the drifting community of the sea.

A drop of sea water taken from the tow-net test tube and examined with the microscope show a scene of intense activity. Creatures of the most bizarre structure wriggle, swim, or dart, into view, and in a

A shoal of small fish streams past the softly whirring undersea movie camera.

The chaetadont has needle-like teeth. It is very common on coral reefs.

The fish of coral reefs are startling in their beauty.

A colourful sea slug (nudibranch) crawling over red organ-pipe coral.

The giant mantis prawn (*Squilla*) is armed with exceptionally sharp and powerful pincers.

The hermit crab hides its tender tail in a discarded sea shell.

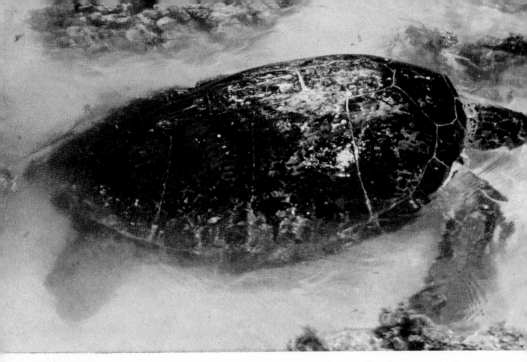

The female green turtle waits in the shallow lagoon for the coming of
night before going ashore to lay her eggs.

The flamboyant beauty of the Butterfly Cod, or Fire Fish (*Pterois volitans*),
masks the poison spines that can cause an agonizing wound.

flash are gone again. Although their progress through the drop of water would appear extremely rapid, it is really of little value in getting them from place to place. For all their excessive energy, so tiny are the microscopic animals that the few inches they may swim are a mere nothing in the immensity of the ocean. As I have said earlier, it is the movement of the currents in the sea that carries them far from their place of origin.

In examining the drop of water one detail is noticeable: the great majority of these creatures that dart so erratically about are crustaceans. So are the crabs and lobsters—but do not think these minute specks are similar in appearance to these two large members of the Crustacea. These microscopic Crustacea are translucent, and their internal organs can be plainly seen through their transparent shells. As they seize some morsel of food, one can see it being torn to pieces in the jaws, and can follow the progress as it is swallowed, digested in the stomach, and the residue eliminated. Even the eggs can be seen forming, and the young developing in the bodies of the animals.

Zoea is a quaint little member of the plankton; it is obviously another crustacean, but like none that can be seen with the unaided eye. Sharp spines project from the back of the head, but are dwarfed by the fearsome lance that projects before it. Its long flexible tail strikes the water with powerful blows, causing the creature to progress in a series of spasmodic leaps.

Swimming beside it is another queer-looking creature, not unlike a squat, transparent lobster. It was named megalopa by the first students of the microscopic life of the sea, but now we know that it is really a zoea, which after several moultings develops into a megalopa. But megalopa itself is still but a baby. As zoea moults and develops into a megalopa, so the latter moults and develops into a baby crab! The three creatures labelled by the early naturalists as zoea, megalopa, and the crab, have now been proved to be but progressive larval stages in the life history of the one animal. Zoea is now known as merely the zoea stage in the life history of a crab.

The mistake made by these early men of science is not to be wondered at. If you have seen even a fraction of the teeming microscopic life of the seas, you will realize what difficulties must be surmounted, and how long and patient the research must be before the life histories of these creatures can be accurately recorded. Few of the young larval creatures of the sea bear the slightest resemblance to their parents, so the only certain method of tracing their life histories is to breed the creatures under laboratory conditions. This means securing the adult animals when they have fertilized eggs in their ovaries. The creatures are then kept in tanks of sea water where conditions must be maintained approximating as closely as possible to the natural environment.

When the eggs or young are ejected, they must be removed to new tanks and kept under close observation, while all stages of their growth are carefully recorded. Then again, when a living specimen of a suspected new species has been captured, it must be kept alive and carefully observed as it develops. We may find that some weird-looking creature—cherished as a strange new specimen—is the baby of some inhabitant of the sea quite familiar to us all. This procedure sounds quite easy, but often the creatures die with their life histories uncompleted: some unknown condition has inhibited further development, and that inhibitory condition must be overcome and the work commenced all over again.

Nearly everyone who has visited the sea-shore knows the jellyfish. It is 99 per cent water, and a goodly part of the remaining one per cent is sheer delicate beauty. From the tow-net test tube I place under the microscope a tiny jelly-fish called a hydro-medusa which makes the most delicately beautiful of the jelly-fish you have seen with the unaided eye quite a coarse material creature in comparison. The one beneath my microscope is surely moulded from plastic crystal—a creature of exquisite loveliness and fragility. With rhythmic pulsations it glides across the field of the microscope to send a volley of poisoned darts into some other inhabitant of this drop of water. The poison brings instant paralysis; for all its fairylike appearance this jelly-fish is a carnivorous animal that devours its paralysed victims. Within the transparent body of the jelly-fish may be seen the eggs that are fertilized by a male of the species.

So far this has been quite an ordinary life history, but now let us see what happens when those developing eggs are set free in the water. They now bear the same name as the baby corals, planulae, and like them are covered with vibrating hairs, which are used as rapidly moving paddles to propel them through the water. These planulae eventually find a suitable place on seaweed, rock, shell, or some other support, and affix themselves firmly to it. The baby of the jelly-fish now grows into what would appear to be a tiny tree with a trunk, and branches growing out from it. Studded along these branches are minute crystal goblets of wonderful transparency, and in each goblet is a single fragile flower. Let us study these flowers under the microscope. Here surely is absurdity, for the petals are in constant movement, and the little blooms continually open and close! Although they resemble flowers they are hungry little animals called hydranths that reach out with poison-laden tentacles to sting and devour the minute life in the waters about them.

This is a colony of hydroids, the parent—or child—of the jelly-fish; you may decide which for yourself, for the story is not yet ended. The hydroid colony develops apace, growing more branches upon which more little hydranths bloom. Then one day, from the trunk or branches of the colony, buds sprout which do not grow into the flower-like hydranths, but into jelly-fish. The members of the hydroid colony have not mated, yet they have borne their children, or if not their children, at least the parents of other hydroid colonies to be; soon the young jelly-fish break free and set out to roam the sea with the plankton, there to meet their mates, for only in this jelly-fish stage are the creatures sexually mature. From that mating again commences this strange cycle of alternating generations, where the children do not resemble their parents, but their grandparents. What patient research it must have needed to discover that a free swimming jelly-fish roaming the seas, and a plant-like colony of animals living permanently attached to the sea-floor or seaweed, were one and the same species!

In the tow-net hauls we find many of the lowly Protozoa, the one-celled organisms. The most striking in appearance is perhaps the Radiolaria. Each is but a mere speck of protoplasm comprising one minute cell, and yet it is able to extract silica from the sea water and manufacture a shell of rare and symmetrical beauty. Each shell is so minute that it would take a million of them to fill a lady's thimble.

Unlike the diatom, the radiolarian is more beautiful when it is alive. The protoplasm reaches out through innumerable apertures in the shell forming a halo of threads as fine as gossamer. These threads fulfil the same purpose as the web of a spider, for they are a net spread to catch its food. In past ages, the Radiolaria, like the diatoms, lived in enormous numbers in the sea, and eventually became compacted into stone; fossil specimens found in the ancient stones are similar to those found living in the seas today.

Another of the Protozoa family, the Foraminifera, build lovely shells, but unlike the diatoms and the Radiolaria, the Foraminifera use carbonate of lime instead of silica as the building material. Some of the shells have tiny apertures dotting their surfaces through which the creature protrudes a web of fine threads of protoplasm. Other species build a shell without the small apertures, but with large doorways from which are protruded a number of threadlike pseudopodia (false feet) which are used to capture food. The Foraminifera multiply by budding one from the other. From the first tiny speck of protoplasm in its minute shell develops a small protuberance that grows larger and builds a shell for itself upon the shell of the first. From this second organism buds another, and so on, all remaining united by a thin thread of protoplasm. This results in some cases in a conglomeration of shells called *Globigerina* which, despite the minute size of each individual shell, form oozes feet deep on parts of the ocean bed. In another species each new shell develops along the same line as the previous one, resulting in a structure of symmetrical form. The shells are very fragile and, if dilute acetic acid is carefully used, can be completely dissolved away, leaving the bodies of the Protozoa almost unchanged and their anatomy plainly displayed.

Fragile as these shells are, ancient Foraminifera are also represented in enormous numbers in the stones of today for they too have fallen to the sea-floor to become compacted and eventually lifted above the sea. I have still to read the "Ode to a Diatom", but I have read a poem, "The White Cliffs", that refers indirectly to the minute shells of the Foraminifera: those famous cliffs are made of chalk, and chalk is composed of the shells of the Foraminifera.

It may surprise many users of some toothpowders to learn that they are cleaning their teeth with the remains of creatures that lived in the sea many thousands, perhaps millions, of years ago. The chalk in those powders is composed almost entirely of fossil Foraminifera.

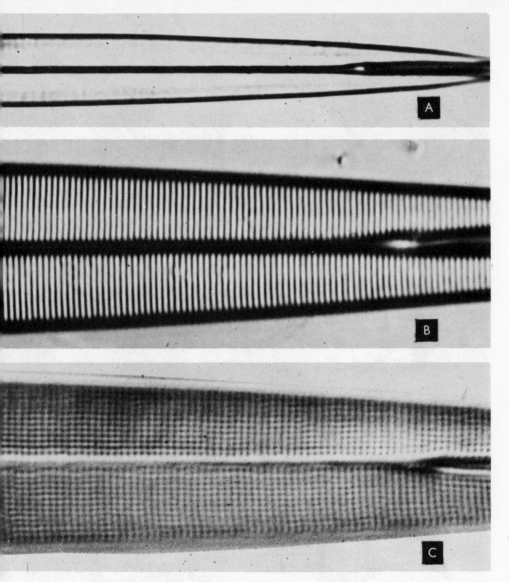

An example of the work that fascinates the "diatomaniac"
in his study of the structure of diatoms.

(A) This diatom was named *Amphipleura pellucida* for, unlike most diatoms, it appeared clear and without markings even when examined with the highest power of the microscope. (B) When the microscope is used with great skill the diatom is no longer pellucid, but appears to be covered with straight lines. So fine are these lines that they can be seen only when using a very good lens. (C) When using such a fine lens, the skilled microscopist can show that the lines are not the real structure; actually they are rows of dots that are so minute that twelve billion one hundred million of these dots would cover an area of only one square inch.

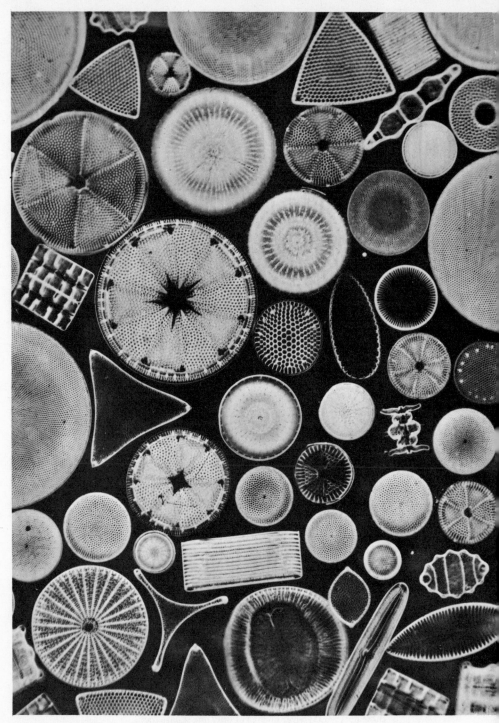

Diatoms—so tiny that it would take a million of them to fill a teaspoon.
(Photo-micrograph from the film *Secrets of the Sea*.)

The Pastures of the Sea

Although many living specimens may be taken in the tow-net, the more usual place to search for them is in the ripples left on the sands by the receding tides. So light are these fairy-like shells, that they are among the last things to be deposited on the sand. To collect them do not go to work with a spade, but with a thin piece of celluloid such as a piece of photographic film. The lightest of touches, a mere surface skimming of the sand, is all that must be taken. Put that surface skimming of dust-like appearance beneath the microscope, and with a hair barely moistened by the tongue, you may pick out many beautiful specimens of these frail shells.

The leisurely movements of diatoms, Radiolaria and Foraminifera, when living, are apt to cause them to be passed over for the other dancing, scintillating life beneath the microscope. There is something so fascinating about the rush and bustle of this life that one can spend hours watching it, not always with the serious purpose of research, but simply as a spectator watching the doings of busier creatures.

Plankton is, as a general rule, much more plentiful in the colder seas, but here it has nothing like the variety of the life found in the Plankton of tropic seas; nor do the creatures from the colder waters have, as a rule, the beauty of those found in warmer seas. There is a reason for this: cold water has more viscosity. In other words, compared to hot water, cold water could be likened to treacle, and, because of this "clinging" property of cold water, an object immersed in it sinks more slowly than it does in water at a higher temperature. This has a direct bearing in tropic seas on modifications in the structure of planktonic animals, for the majority of them live their lives comparatively near the surface of the sea; and, since the warm tropic seas have less viscosity, the planktonic life must be specially adapted to such conditions or it would sink much too speedily and the tiny creatures would perish in a hopeless effort to keep up. Therefore they are often adorned with appendages such as long spines, and their antennae and tails are embellished with long, fine hairs. These gives them a most spectacular appearance, for the fringing hairs are like feathery plumes bedecking their minute bodies. The purpose of these ornate trimmings is to keep them nearer the surface, for each plume-like appendage "clings" to the water, and so reduces the sinking speed.

Microscopic plants must live where the rays of the sun can reach the chlorophyll in their cells, and since these be-plumed creatures feed upon the plants, or perhaps eat other creatures that feed on the plants, they have developed in this way to ensure that they can remain at the surface in the vicinity of their food-supply.

Do not think, however, that the plankton is found only where air and water meet; this is a matter of comparison. You could say with truth that you lived in the mountains without your home being perched upon the summit. A surface haul of the tow-net during the day may come up almost empty, but if the net is allowed to sink down a few feet farther it may come up with the test tube teeming with life. It is a peculiarity of the planktonic creatures that the different members of that community seem to prefer varying intensities of light, and many shun the full glare of sunlight. During the day they sink deeper until they reach a level where the light filtering down from above has just the degree of intensity that they prefer. So, during the day the sea contains layers of planktonic life; those preferring comparative darkness are lower down, and the layers progress upwards according to the light intensity preferred by each kind of animal. As the sun passes its zenith and its rays strike the surface of the sea at a progressively oblique angle, the plankton begins to rise, still attempting to remain in water which has the intensity of light each species prefers. The nearer the sun approaches the west, the higher rises the plankton, until shortly before sunset and during the night the upper waters of the sea are populated with a swarming multitude of microscopic animals. In another chapter ("Architects and Artisans of the Reef") we found that many of the coral polyps emerge to feed only at night, and herein lies the explanation of this habit. Their meals would be scanty indeed if they fed only in the day-time, for coral grows only in comparatively shallow waters, and during the day the microplankton upon which the polyps feed would have escaped the brilliant light of day by sinking farther into the depths. Only with the setting sun does it rise to the surface where the currents may sweep it in over the coral reefs.

The life of the sea would seem to be a well-ordered community. Many of the creatures that in adulthood live their lives in the depths give birth to young that are free-swimming; the young, instead of preferring the shadowy depths, rise to the brighter regions above to join the community of the plankton where the currents carry them far from the place of their birth. Free-swimming seeds of seaweeds (zoospores) also rise to the upper regions and are distributed in the same way. If the young animals lived their lives where they were born, it is obvious that such localities would soon become overcrowded, and eventually the creatures in that area would almost die out because of the superabundance of hungry mouths.

One night I was lured out on the reef more by the beauty of the lagoon in the moonlight than by the hope of a successful catch of microscopic life, for I have found that there is often a scarcity of plankton in the shallow waters of the lagoon when the moon is at its full. As the boat drifted across the submerged reef, a shadowy shoal of fish sped silently by. Then it seemed as if the shoal had entered a city, for brilliant lights flashed out wherever the shoal moved. It was a ghostly bluish light, although extremely brilliant, and the scales of the fish threw back the glare in gleaming reflections.

This was worth investigating, and down went the plankton net. As it was drawn up through the water it borrowed some of the brilliance of that blue illumination for its conical shape was outlined in fire. On examining the water in the test tube at the bottom of the plankton net, fine white threads could be seen darting with wriggling undulations through the water. As I looked over the side of the boat I could see the lights rising to the surface, and soon the water surrounding us was flashing with a myriad of erratic rockets. Leaning overboard, I scooped some of this glowing water up in my hand, which then glowed as if it too were dipped in liquid fire, and for some time afterwards whatever I touched glowed with a ghostly light.

Returning to the laboratory I placed a drop of water, with several of the fine threads wriggling through it, upon the slide of the microscope. Those darting threads were tiny marine worms which now took on the formidable proportions of fabled sea-serpents. The little creatures swam with the vigorous paddling of an army of bristle-tipped legs. When they developed top speed, the wriggling of their bodies was so fast that each creature appeared as a white blur.

There was a reason for this tremendous activity: the worms were spawning. I turned out the light in the laboratory and watched the marriage ceremony by the creatures' own light. As the females reached the top speed of their wriggling they emitted a cloud of luminous eggs through which the male worms dashed ejecting streams of sperms. Under a higher powered lens I watched the minute sperms with rapid wriggling of their long whip-like tails swim to the luminous eggs and fertilize them. Even though they were but worms, I felt privileged to be present at their nuptials.

Many a time I have seen the waters surrounding our coral island gleam with this glory of liquid fire, for a great many of the sea creatures are luminous, a power they share with glow-worms, and fire-flies. This lighting up of the sea is generally called phosphorescence, but it would be more correct to call it luminescence, for the light is not caused by phosphorus, which is a powerful poison and would quickly destroy the creatures. It is a much more subtle means of creating light. This light is brilliant and yet gives out no heat. Man has not yet discovered the secret of a cold light for his own use. There is an instrument called the bolometer which is so sensitive that it can be used to register the heat coming from distant stars. Not even the extreme sensitivity of the bolometer can show that the light emitted by these creatures possesses the tiniest proportion of heat rays. An American physiologist, Professor E. Newton Harvey, has discovered that this light is produced as a result of the oxidization of a substance called luciferin that glows when combined with oxygen. But this action cannot take place unless another substance called luciferase is present. Here is mystery upon mystery, for the luminous creatures have the power of allowing the luciferase to mix with the luciferin and oxygen, and so produce the brilliant light by oxidization; but the luciferase without which this action cannot take place remains quite unoxidized and unaltered. It would appear to act merely as a kind of lubricant which allows the phenomenon to take place smoothly, but does not combine with either luciferin or oxygen. The purpose of this brilliant illumination in the creatures of the sea would, in many cases, seem to have no useful purpose, although in some cases it may act as a lure in attracting small creatures for food.

The sea is like a book with many pages. The print on some of these pages is exceedingly small, and if you would read the absorbing stories on the pages with small print a microscope becomes a necessity.

CHAPTER 12

ACCIDENTS WILL HAPPEN

THIS life we have chosen has only one serious disadvantage: a submerged but ever-present anxiety that accident or sickness may overtake one or both of us when we are in the depths of the jungle, or on some isolated, uninhabited island far from medical aid. Risks are inseparable from the type of work we do, and although we try to avoid unnecessary dangers they cannot always be foreseen. The desire to photograph some particular scene or subject is so apt temporarily to put the sense of judgment into abeyance, and then only chance or good luck can save the day.

As Kitty says, usually after the event: "You and your one-track mind! How do you think I would feel being left all alone? If you die under the sea I might not see even your body again, and if we are in the jungle, am I to dig a grave and bury you there, then try to find my way out alone?" Listening in submissive silence, I know she is right to scold me: but awkward situations seem silently to creep up on one, and to become evident only as *faits accomplis*.

Wearing the aqualung, I was swimming along the inner edge of a coral reef with my winged undersea camera. A big shoal of rainbow-hued parrot-fish sped out from a deep canyon in the coral reef. They made a glorious picture as, brightly lit, they swam in the open sea with the sombre gloom of the canyon as a background. Tilting the wings of the camera, I swam downwards towards them. As I approached they turned back towards the reef and disappeared into a deep narrow channel. They were swimming leisurely, so I knew they had not been frightened by my approach, and I swam into the channel after them in the hope that they would again swim out into the open where I could get a good picture. As I swam forward, the channel grew narrower overhead, and I realized it was becoming a tunnel under the coral. There was a turn just a short distance ahead, and I decided to swim round the corner, and, if the parrot-fish had disappeared, return again to the inner edge of the reef.

I turned the corner and it was like looking along a tube. At the far end was the lovely translucent blue of the open sea with the parrot-fish moving slowly past. It looked too good to miss, so I swam on down the tunnel. When I reached the opening the shoal had moved some distance away, so again I followed them out into the open, intent on securing my picture. They still showed no sign of fear, but most tantalizingly stayed just out of range for a good under-sea picture. One of the great difficulties in underwater photography is to get close enough to the subject to overcome the mistiness caused by the sediment and microscopic life in the sea.

Concentration on the job prevented my noticing a dull, rhythmic, thudding sound, and it was only when the shoal moved steadily away into the distance that I realized the sound had been going on for some time. It is very difficult to identify sounds under the sea, so I swam upwards towards the surface. As I ascended, the sea became very bright, but so full of air bubbles it was impossible to see where I was going. Then my head broke the surface, and I struck out desperately to escape being dashed by the waves onto the reef. I was on the outer edge of the reef where the breakers from the open sea were pounding down on to the coral, and the tide had turned and was sweeping in over the exposed reef. That submarine tunnel I had come through ran from the smooth water in the lee of the reef to the open water of the Coral Sea. Kitty and the dinghy were on the other side of the reef in the sheltered water, and there was no way for her to reach me even if the dinghy could have remained afloat in those angry seas. If I tried to swim with the incoming tide across the shallow reef I would be torn to pieces on the coral; the only hope was to find that many-times accursed tunnel, and return the way I had come. I had come out of the tunnel and followed the fish to the right of the opening.

Down I went into the quiet water beneath the churning seas, and swam in again towards the cliff-like face of the reef. As I swam, I realized I should have known where I was as soon as I came out of the tunnel, for now I was near the reef I could see the cliff face going sheer down until it faded away into the awesome blue of the depths. There was nothing between me and the floor of the sea but several thousand feet of deep blue ocean. The continental shelf ends abruptly beyond the northern Outer Reef, but the sea inside the Great

Barrier Reef is comparatively shallow: reef-building corals cannot grow at a depth of more than one hundred and fifty feet. Sheer carelessness—I should have known better than to allow my interest in obtaining one not very important shot to put me in this predicament.

Steadily I swam along, keeping the face of the submarine cliff on my left. The tunnel opening must now be near. I saw an opening and struck out more strongly. It looked like the tunnel. I paused and peered into the opening. No, that's not it; it is evidently only a deep cave; the coral walls disappear into darkness, and there is no sign of light shining through from the other end in the lee of the reef. I swam on. Another opening—well, that was lucky, it didn't take long to find. But this was not it, only a coral grotto extending back twenty or thirty feet into the cliff face. I began to swim faster. How many false openings would I have to explore before finding the right one? I began to breathe heavily. Steady up—the faster you swim, the more air you'll use up. This is a time to keep cool—I feel cold. Calm—that was the word—keep calm—things are bad enough without starting to panic. I wonder how much compressed air remains in these steel bottles? Forget it—you can't put any more in now. Where is that tunnel? I must have passed it—I've come a good deal farther along this way than when I followed that shoal of fish. You fool! Of course you have—that wasn't a cave you passed the first time, that was the tunnel! Don't you remember the turn near the other end? Of course the light doesn't show through—how do you think the light can turn corners? Round I swung and started back. The entrance! It looks familiar, but I could be wrong. Well, if I am wrong—I could be dead. In I go.

The light grew dimmer as I swam inwards until I could barely see the walls of jagged coral, which seemed to be slipping past me at an ever-increasing speed. Fear gives wings to one's feet, so I have heard. I seemed to be doing quite well with ordinary rubber flippers on my feet. Very dark now. Then I realized why I was moving so fast. I was in the tunnel all right, but the incoming tide was racing through it like a mill race! If I touched the sides of the tunnel I would have only a short period to appreciate what "death by a thousand cuts" meant. The air was coming feebly from my bottles, and I pulled the emergency wire which releases a last five minutes of air. Then I saw a wall of coral rapidly growing nearer and brighter—the turn in the tunnel! I swam hard towards the right-hand side so that I could turn sharp around the corner. It was bright and clear now. I reached the turn and swam strongly forward towards the exit, but the racing waters carried me towards the wall on the left. Frantically I lashed out with my flippers. Almost round. An agonizing pain bit into my leg. I had kicked savagely against a jagged mass of branching coral. Forget it—keep kicking! I was round the turn and speeding towards the calm water inside the reef. Leg was a bit sore—but not too bad—my emergency air supply was still functioning smoothly—I surfaced and swam towards Kitty and the dinghy.

When we got back to the camp, I found that two spear-points of coral had broken off and were deeply embedded in the flesh of my leg. I dug the coral out, washed the wound thoroughly, stitched it, and thought no more about it. It soon closed up and gave me no bother.

Two or three weeks later I woke during the night with a dull throbbing in my leg. The wound was practically healed, but the leg looked a little swollen. In the morning it was aching with a steady nagging persistence. There was nothing in the appearance of the leg to cause alarm. No sign of angry red around the almost healed scar. Just a slight swelling and a nagging ache that was forgotten as soon as I started the day's work. That evening, while Kitty was preparing a meal, I brought in an armful of firewood. Kitty watched me as I walked towards her.

"One of your legs looks thicker than the other," she said.

"It is the one I cut on the coral; it swelled up a bit," I replied.

"So I see." She pushed her cooking on one side and put water on to heat. "Dinner can wait. Hot fomentations for you, my lad."

We always take with us a good medical kit, so while the water was heating I prepared the hypodermic with a massive dose of penicillin, jabbed in the needle, and took a couple of sulpha tablets for good measure. So began some agonizing weeks. The leg continued to swell until it was a burden to carry around with me. The only relief was getting into the sea with the camera each day. Then the bouyancy of the water seemed to relieve some of the feeling of oppressive weight in that aching leg. There was also the compensation of knowing that I was getting some good film, for it was spring, and the sea was teeming with life. But those nights! Fitful snatches of sleep—hours of lying awake waiting for the sunrise with a leg that felt as if some heavily panting animal was gnawing at it!

One night I flipped a cigarette end out into the darkness in front of the tent. Idly I watched the little spurt of sparks as it landed on the sand; then it came rapidly back into the tent and came towards me like a growing, malevolent eye! A nice state of affairs—now I was becoming delirious! Then the glowing eye began to move around in an erratic pattern on the sand beside my camp bed. I reached down to pick it up. It darted away to elude my clutching fingers. No doubt about it—delirium! Kitty woke when she heard me muttering to myself.

"What's the matter?" she said, sleepily.

Trying to speak nonchalantly, I answered, "I think I dropped a cigarette beside my bed, can you see. . . ?"

Kitty interrupted. "Ooher!—what's that thing moving about down there?"

"See something?" I remarked through a hastily devised yawn.

"There's a horrible red eye just gone under my bed," said Kitty indignantly.

Very interesting—epidemic delirium.

"Oh bother!" I could hear Kitty fumbling for the electric torch on the box between our beds, then a triumphant "Ah!"

The "evil eye" darted out again from under her bed. On went the torch.

A sand crab, waving its eye stalks in a semaphore greeting, stood in the circle of light solemnly holding aloft in one nipper—my glowing cigarette butt!

In some of the nights that followed, I was grateful to that crazy little crab that had carried a torch for me. When the pain was too bad to allow sleep, I would creep out of bed and, taking the torch, would wander down to the beach to study the nightly doings of these queer crustaceans.

They are of the half-way place between sea and land creatures, and are evolving into completely terrestrial animals. The gills their ancestors possessed have become so modified that they are now primitive lungs and breathe air. It seems necessary for them still to live close to the sea, for periodically they come out of their burrows in the sand and scamper down the beach into the sea, where they remain for only a few seconds before coming out again. Evidently they must still keep their lungs wet in order that their breathing apparatus may function efficiently. They emerge from their burrows only at night, and are commonly called ghost crabs. Pale as a corpse, they do have a ghostly appearance as, on tip-toe, they move across the sand at amazing speed looking as unsubstantial as drifting shadows.

Sitting quietly on the beach one could imagine that one was on the bank of some woodland pool peopled by a myriad of tiny frogs as the queer, croaking noises made by the crabs in their burrows rose in a muffled chorus. Perhaps this is a love call? I singled out one burrow from which arose a steady croaking, and watched another crab drift across the sand to the entrance, then scuttle down the passage. The croaking suddenly increased in volume, with perhaps a tone of indignation, and out darted the visitor. I caught it, and it was a male crab. Maybe a rejected suitor. I watched again. Another visitor. Same hurried exit. Another male. A fastidious lady, perhaps. Yet another visitor, and this one remained. Is it a male or female visitor who has remained down the burrow? I cannot say. Perhaps the owner of the burrow is a male calling to a female: he would very naturally resent the intrusion of the two males. If so, perhaps the last visitor who has remained there is a female, and a honeymoon is in progress. Who knows! The sand still holds the secret.

Although their love life is obscure, there is no doubt about the efficiency of the ghost crabs as scavengers. All the flotsam and jetsam stranded on the beach by the outgoing tide is carefully picked over, and any organic matter eaten. Stranded on the beach, a dying fish soon has an eager queue of diners lining up, and even before the last feeble wriggle the ghost crabs are enjoying a fish dinner. Their manner of eating bears an absurd likeness to humans eating in a tremendous hurry, and brings back rueful memories of hasty meals gulped down in Railway Dining Rooms (please note capitals). While one nipper is transferring a morsel of fish to the mouth, the other nipper is tearing off another sliver of fish, and without a pause, as one nipper comes down from the mouth the other nipper is moving up to it. While a meal is in progress the ghost crabs seem a good-natured crowd. Latecomers, finding "all seats taken" would scramble over the backs of the early diners into the centre of the meal and set to with gusto. The incoming tide would submerge a clean picked skeleton.

Strengthened by the meal, the crabs would commence burrow-digging operations. For this work their delicate sharp pointed legs are not adapted, but their big, broad nippers make admirable sand scoops. Occasionally a crab would sidle out the doorway, turn and throw the excavated sand down the beach with the jerky, awkward action of a woman throwing away dirty water from a basin. These crabs have one very disconcerting habit. While I was absorbed in watching one party of workers, there would be a sudden most painful pressure on some part of my bare feet. A crab would be sampling them, and an eager party hurrying to join the feast. Hang it all! I was neither flotsam nor jetsam. They are large crabs with very powerful nippers, and I have no doubt that a badly injured or unconscious man could fare very badly if cast ashore on a beach with a large ghost crab population.

I ceased my crab-watching because of a new interest which took its place during the sleepless nights. That swollen leg had now opened up at the scars where the injury had occurred. During my early married life as a musician I had become deeply interested in bacteriology, and had experimented with the growing of bacteria in test tubes and Petrie dishes. My deepest interest, however, had been in studying their resistance or reaction to different drugs, and in devising new staining methods to assist in the identification of different species of similar outward appearance. In those days most of my spare pocket money was used to acquire finer lenses and accessories for my microscope, but I never seemed to be able to accumulate enough money to purchase everything I longed to buy.

To grow cultures of germs required an incubator, for it is remarkable how delicate and fastidious about their environment these deadly little germs can be. The purchase of an expensive bacteriological incubator would completely upset my budget, yet how otherwise could I keep my cultures at blood heat? Blood heat! I was at blood heat. Small culture tubes were wrapped in lint, and I fastened the little packages on to my body with strips of sticking plaster. This worked beautifully, and I grew fine crops of germs with which to experiment. Each night on going to bed, I would peel off the plaster and put my culture tubes in a flat cotton-wool-lined tin which I kept at night in my pyjama pocket. Then, a few moments of forgetfulness brought tragedy. One morning I forgot to take the tubes from the tin and fasten them to my skin. Kitty saw the tin in my pyjama pocket, opened it, and saw the array of little glass tubes all so neatly labelled with names that left no doubt as to their contents. Kitty was really upset. No explanations sufficed. I was no longer to be a perambulating germ incubator.

That seemed that, but all was not lost. Before Kitty's discovery of my bottled companions, I had devised a method which, instead of staining bacteria with a colour of even density, which is usual with the standard stains, gave a delicate stain that had a greater affinity with some elements than with others within the cell walls of these minute organisms. Beneath the highest power of the microscope, with this method of staining, it was possible to see a hint of structure instead of only the usual blank shape. A paper I had written regarding this method and illustrated with lantern slide photomicrographs had been presented to a scientific society. One of the members who had been at the presentation called at our home to have me demonstrate the method to him. Now that I was no longer allowed to be an incubator I had no germs to show him. Kitty explained why. Our visitor was much amused, but had a solution. He was a doctor, and the Superintendent of one of the largest hospitals in Sydney. He would arrange for me to continue with my experiments in a corner of the hospital laboratory, and a place in the incubator would be found for my wogs.

Those were joyous days. I worked in the laboratory in the morning, and departed just in time to reach the theatre before the overture commenced. The technician in charge of the laboratory found time during his busy days to instruct me in the routine and methods adopted in a pathological laboratory. A theatrical tour in the orchestra of the Pavlova ballet company forced me reluctantly to leave the laboratory, but now, with a leg apparently as well stocked as the laboratory incubator, I could once more do some study on wogs.

It is rather surprising to discover how many people imagine bacteria to be malevolent little animals, which, finding an entry into the body, bare savage fangs and start in to eat up the blood corpuscles and other body cells. The dangerous bacteria are only in a small minority amongst the family of the bacteria. Also, they are not animals but minute one-celled plants; and they do not eat our tissues, but kill them with poisonous substances that are a by-product of their own metabolism. If their Borgia-like behaviour causes our death, another kind of bacteria takes over, the putrefactive bacteria, which return our tissues to their primary elements. Under such conditions the pathogenic bacteria cannot live, so they perish also. Some dangerous germs however, leave spores, seeds that may lie dormant for long periods, but again develop into killers when conditions are suitable. The anthrax bacillus is one of these dangerous spore-bearers.

The fatal power of these most minute plants is not in the potency of the poison of the individual bacterium; it is in the almost unbelievable speed of their ability to multiply. They grow by one individual dividing into two. This division can, under ideal conditions, take place every thirty minutes, and so their numbers become prodigious in but a few hours. If there is nothing to hinder their growth one bacterium can give rise to a family of over 200 million millions in a period of twenty-four hours! Under normal circumstances there is a limit to the continued multiplication of bacteria; the death of their host creates an environment unsuitable for their further increase. Some species of bacteria are aerobic, which means that they can grow only when oxygen is present; anaerobic bacteria can live only where there is no oxygen; while some species are indifferent to the presence or the lack of air. Direct sunlight is fatal to most pathogenic bacteria in a very short time, since they cannot withstand the effect of the violet end of the spectrum. Ordinary window glass absorbs ultra-violet light, and bacteria can continue to live in a room brightly lit by the sun shining through the windows, but the same bacteria would die in a short time if placed outside. Other factors also make it impossible for bacteria to go on increasing in numbers. If one can imagine one bacterium being in a situation where there was nothing to curb its ability to multiply, theoretically in five days the result could be a mass of bacteria larger than the earth! To make the marvel even more astounding, consider the size of these extraordinary and potent plants. The surface of a one-inch postage stamp could accommodate 5,125,000,000 bacteria, and then they would be in a layer of only $\frac{1}{25,000}$ of an inch in thickness—or thinness. It is the combined poison of their countless billions that causes illness or death. There is yet another marvel that should be recognized: the ability of man to make instruments and lenses of such precision that these minute organisms can be seen and studied.

Bacteria are not the only organisms dangerous to man. Protozoa, microscopic animals, are also killers. Malaria and sleeping sickness are two well-known diseases caused by protozoa, and there are other dangers for mankind in plants that have evolved into a higher form of plant life than that of the simple bacteria. These higher forms are minute mould-like plants, which can also cause painful and fatal diseases. Another family of our minute enemies are too small to be seen through the visual microscope. They are the invisible viruses: strange and little understood organisms that would seem to have some characteristics of inorganic matter, rather than life as we understand life.

My microscopic examination showed that only bacteria were having fun and games in my leg, so I attacked them with massive doses of penicillin and sulpha drugs. Most septic wounds have quite a garden plot of different species of bacteria, but every night my microscope showed a most gratifying reduction in the number of species living in the wound. However, there was one type of bacteria living on undaunted by the drugs, and it was present in enormous numbers. No drug it seemed could kill this hardy invader, and to make things more annoying I could not identify it.

Then a doctor on a fishing vacation visited our lonely island. He was deeply interested in the whole affair, but gave me a nasty jolt with his diagnosis.

"Those pieces of coral that drove in there have pierced the bone. This is a bone infection. I'll take my boat straight back to the mainland and put you into hospital."

"How long in hospital?" I asked.

"Oh, if everything goes O.K. about two or three months. Leg must go into plaster, irrigation tubes, we'll fix you up all right, its only a matter of. . . ."

"No hospital," I interrupted.

"You don't seem to realize just how serious this is. If that infection is not cleared up, you can lose your leg, or even your life," he replied, in a rather annoyed tone.

"Now wait a minute," I said, apologetically. "I am in an awkward position. I have signed a contract with an American film company to produce the film we are working on, and two or three months in hospital would mean the season will be over, and we shall have completely upset the plans of our American contractors."

The doctor said nothing, so I continued more hopefully.

"The other wogs that were in that leg are practically gone; sulpha or penicillin fixed them. Now if there is some drug that would knock out this obstinate type, I could continue with my work."

The doctor considered for a few minutes.

"Here's what we do. Give me a sterile test tube with a swab from that leg. I've got to go back to the mainland for further supplies, and tomorrow I'll put the tube on the plane for immediate delivery to the Public Health Laboratories in Brisbane. We'll see if they can identify the wog and send back something that will wipe it out. If it isn't successful within a reasonably short time—hospital."

His boat disappeared in the direction of the mainland, and I got busy with the cameras so I would not have to meet Kitty's accusing eyes. She had been trying to persuade me to go to the mainland each time our supply boat called.

A few days later, we were just about to sit down to dinner when we heard a boat engine. The good-natured doctor had come back with the laboratory report and—chloromycetin. The laboratory had been unable to identify the bacteria, but they had found what would destroy them. The doctor would not even wait until dinner was over, but got to work.

The next few days he spent fishing around the island, and we shared a session with the microscope each night before I went to bed —and to sleep. I was almost afraid to believe what seemed to be happening. One night he looked up from the microscope.

"Did you search through this slide?"

"Yes," I replied, and put three more slides down alongside the microscope. "I searched these three also—nothing."

He gave a satisfied nod, then, "Well, suppose we have a rum before we turn in," he said.

It turned into one of those nights when we had several rums.

The scars will always remain. So will the memory of a good friend.

CHAPTER 13

WE TURN NIGHT INTO DAY

THOROUGHLY disgruntled, I sat in the shade. For several days I had been an exile from the sea. I had finished doing all the odd jobs I could find around the camp—oiled the cameras, cleaned microscope and camera lenses, made up fresh photographic solutions—and there seemed to be nothing else to do but sit round and mope. Certainly, the infection was cleaned up, and my leg no longer throbbed with pain, nor did it now look as if it would have been more appropriate to an elephant; but I might just as well be in hospital as loafing around the camp all day.

Before departing, the doctor had ordered dry dressings, and no sea water until the skin had closed over the two raw cavities that still gaped but were filling in rapidly. Temperate seas have the reputation of possessing healing properties; but there is not the slightest doubt that this is not the case with the warm sea water of the Great Barrier Reef. Superficial cuts remain open for weeks if one spends many hours of each day in the sea, and deeper wounds are peculiarly apt to become septic. I wanted nothing more to do with sepsis, but I did want film in the box.

Kitty must have heard my impatient snort, for she looked up from her book.

"Don't be a grizzle-pot—you've earned a rest. Would you like to read one of these books the doctor left?"

"No thanks," I said hastily. "I'll read it later."

I had no wish to read. I wanted to be down with my camera in that fascinating blue world I could see shimmering so tantalizingly through the fringe of coconut palms. Then my eyes caught sight of the really resplendent fly of our tent. Now, there was something interesting, and it could mean useful scenes for our film.

Before coming to this island I had purchased a new tent-fly. Kitty's housewifely pride had been obvious as she looked approvingly at the

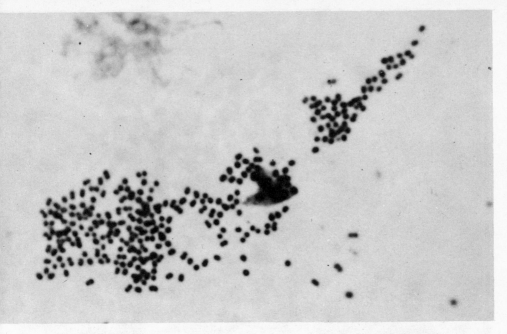

Bacteria (extremely minute primitive plants, some of which cause disease). These unidentified micrococci (superficially resembling staphylococci) nearly cost the author his leg. (Highly magnified.)

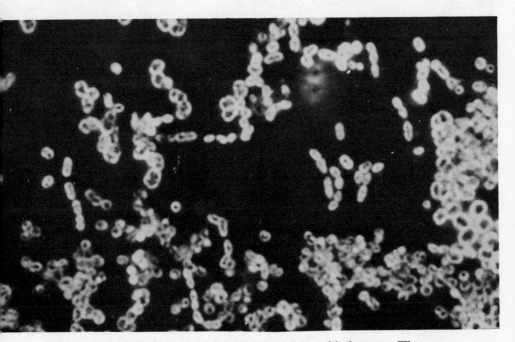

All our lives we are surrounded by billions of invisible bacteria. These are living bacteria in the saliva from a healthy mouth. (Highly magnified.)

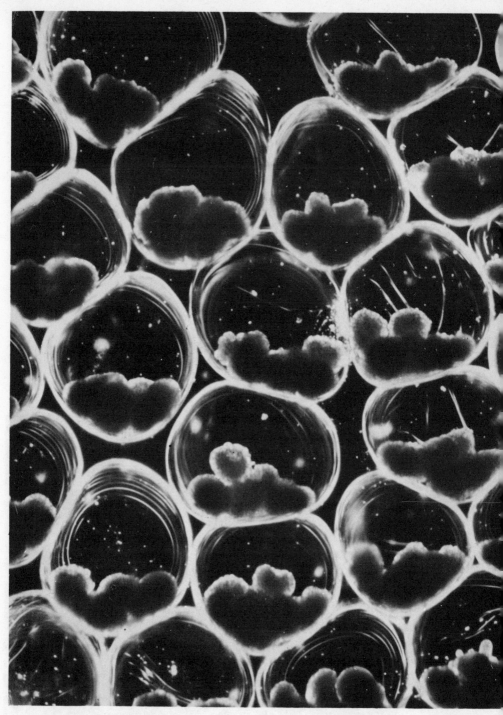

The eggs of the nudibranch are laid in a delicate ribbon containing up to half a million embryos. (Highly magnified; micro-photograph from the film *Secrets of the Sea.*)

immaculate white canvas stretched above the tent. The next morning she had looked with dismay at the bright purple stains that turned the fly into a piebald monstrosity. It was not until the next night that I discovered the cause of the gaudy coloration. Our camp was surrounded by native plum-trees, heavily laden with fruit. At night hordes of flying-foxes descended on the trees to gorge on the plums. Mixed with the digestive juices in the stomachs of the flying-foxes, the fruit juices were converted into an indelible dye. Further observations proved that in regard to their intestinal contents flying-foxes are constitutionally careless. However, Kitty need not have worried unduly about the piebald appearance. Within a week our new tent-fly was no longer piebald, but as rich a royal purple as the toga of a Roman emperor.

I was collecting my camera gear before Kitty recovered from her surprise at my sudden activity.

"What are you going to do with the cameras?" she said reprovingly. "You musn't go into the water."

"Who wants to go in the water? If we're making a picture of the sea life around coral islands we should also include the creatures that live on the islands. There's one furred animal we haven't used a foot of film on," I said happily.

Kitty looked at me in wonderment. "But there aren't any furred . . . unless you mean those dirty flying-foxes," she replied.

"Of course I mean the flying-foxes. There are no other furred animals that can reach these isolated coral islands under their own power. They belong to this film and must be included."

Kitty was now helping me to get the gear we needed, but she shook her head doubtfully. "But aren't they nocturnal animals? How are we going to make a film of them?"

"We'll get them at home in their colony first," I said, as we started off, "and then I've got another idea that might work."

"But you don't know where they camp in the day-time," she said.

I spoke confidently, hoping I was right. "But I do. I've watched them in the early morning before sunrise. They all fly towards the centre of the island. That's where they camp."

What a scramble that was! As we got nearer the centre of the island we encountered a veritable jungle laced through with a tangled mass of thorny "wait-a-while" vines. Smiling encouragement at each other, we struggled on with the shrill cries of quarrelling flying-foxes only a short distance ahead.

The flying-fox camp was in the top of one of the highest trees on the island. As the tree swayed backwards and forwards in the south-east trade wind, the sunlight gleamed on the golden neck fur of these queer mammals. We were grateful to that wind, for it carried the nauseous stench of the foxes away to be dispersed over the wide sea. Our cameras were soon in action, and all my ill-humour had gone.

Flying-foxes are giant bats with a wingspread of up to four feet, and so powerful is their flight that they have been observed flying over the sea more than two hundred miles from the nearest land. The structure of the wing is interesting. A membrane, like thin, black rubber, is stretched between each "finger" of an enormously elongated "hand". This membrane extends down the side of the body to the hind-legs across which the membrane extends without a break. Unlike the wings of a bird, the membrane continues in one unbroken piece from the extreme tip of the wing on one side to the extreme wing-tip on the other, thus presenting an enormous wing surface in comparison with the size of the body of the animal. While it is sleeping, hanging head downwards in the trees, the wings are wrapped completely around the body, and in the heavy rains of the tropics they must act as a very efficient raincoat and keep the very dark reddish-brown, indeed almost black, fur dry. When moving about in the trees searching for fruit flying-foxes use the equivalent of the thumb in the "hand", which terminates in a long grappling hook. The flying-fox reaches out, hooks on to a branch with its "thumb", and swings through the trees with the speed and agility of a monkey. When it is hanging by its hooked feet to feed on the fruit, the fingers of the wing act like the ribs of a fan and the wings are folded neatly and lie flat alongside the body. They would seem to be the most versatile wings possessed by any flying creature.

Quarrels among the foxes were of frequent occurrence, but were more verbal than physical. One would wake, yawn, then unwind and partly stretch its wings. The outstretched wings would touch sleeping neighbours on each side. The awakened neighbours would stretch their wings with a similar result. Thus a whole group would break into sudden activity amidst a medley of indignant chattering squeals.

Demoniac little faces would wrinkle with fury, beady eyes glare from side to side, the lips would draw back showing formidable rows of sharply pointed white teeth, while threatening squeals rose to a climax. A sudden reshuffle of their positions on a bough would take place, each would glare for a moment at its new neighbour. Then, with the gesture of the conspirator of old melodrama, wrapping his black cape around him and tossing one end over his shoulder, the wings would be folded around their bodies to leave them hanging silently for all the world like a bunch of absurd little Draculas.

We made our way back to the camp in the warm, short twilight of the tropics with the pleasant awareness that the day had supplied a good quota of useful film material. Dinner over, we got down to planning what other scenes would be required to round out the flying-fox sequence. "Fruit and blossom-eating bats" is the natural-history book description of these creatures, but I considered that this was not quite accurate. Certainly there was no doubt about the fruit-eating; and since they had eaten all the ripe native plums they had been swarming into the coral-flower trees (*Erythrina indica*), which were now in full blossom. Hidden in the shadows beneath the trees, I had been watching them through binoculars on a night of full moon, and I doubted that the petals of the flowers were the great attraction. If only I could get a film of the foxes actually eating, I would know.

I explained to Kitty what had caused me to think there was something else than flowers attracting them. When the trees had first shown signs of bursting into bloom, I had visited them each day in order to see them in their full beauty. The blossoms had just opened one day, yet on the very next day the ground beneath the tree was thinly carpeted with fallen petals from the flowers. The next day a red carpet of petals was spread more thickly beneath the tree. The fallen petals were young and fresh, not dry and dead from a withering flower. Watching closely through the binoculars I had seen petals dropping as the foxes commenced to feed. Then the petals ceased to drop, but the foxes seem to be satisfied to remain eating where that flower had been growing, rather than moving to the next flower. So it semed obvious that they sought something more than the fleshy petals.

"Just think, if we could get some pictures with the deep blue of the tropic sky as a background, silhouetting the dark bodies of the feeding flying-foxes with golden manes gleaming in the sun. The stark, leafless branches of the coral-trees bearing aloft their flame-coloured blossoms, and the . . ."

"Steady on!" interrupted Kitty. "I began to lose track of that when you got to that bit about golden manes of feeding flying-foxes gleaming in the sun. Where do you think you are, in the Land of the Midnight Sun?"

"That's the whole point of it," I said excitedly. "If we can only get that picture we've got a naturalist's scoop."

"It certainly would be if we could make moving pictures in the dark," said Kitty witheringly. "How do you think you are going to get these pictures?"

"With an empty kerosene-tin," I replied.

Kitty looked at me scornfully and departed to her bed. But I was not joking.

Early next morning I was hard at work in the centre of the coral tree building a little platform to hold me and the camera. Around this I erected a little room of leafy boughs taken from adjacent trees. The coral-trees shed all their leaves before flowering. I made a small opening in front of the camera lens, and this completed the job.

Back at our camp, I slung the camera bags over my shoulders and, after handing Kitty an empty kerosene-tin, which she took from me without comment, I picked up the two movie tripods and set off for the flying-fox camp. One camera was set up on the flying-foxes asleep in their tree. Then I handed Kitty a good stout stick and said, "We're ready now. I'm going over to the coral-trees to set the other camera up. Give me about twenty minutes to get there and to get ready, switch on the motor of this camera, then beat that tin with the stick. That should wake the flying-foxes, and this camera should get a good picture of them swinging through the branches and launching themselves into the air. Every time they try to land in the tree, chase them away again. Maybe some of them will get tired of flying round and will decide to have a meal at the coral-tree. If they do, I'll be waiting for them with the other camera."

Hidden in my leafy cubby-hole, I heard the faint banging on the tin and watched eagerly for flying-foxes. Time went by, but no flying-foxes appeared. Several times I heard Kitty banging away at her tin then silence—hours of silence, but no flying-foxes.

The sun had set before I pushed my way through the thick under-growth towards the flying-fox camp. When she heard me saying rude things about spiky and clinging lawyer-vines, a tired and bored little Kitty called out hopefully, "Did you get them?"

I tore free from the last lawyer-vine to find Kitty sitting on the battered tin, and shook my head.

"Never saw one," I said miserably.

"It was a good idea if it had worked," said Kitty comfortingly.

I lay awake for a time that night wondering what had gone wrong. Even if the foxes would not bother about having their breakfast before the sun set, I had at least expected to see them flying round above the coral-trees.

Morning brought renewed confidence. Where had the flying-foxes gone when Kitty scared them from their camp? I would not be satis-fied until I knew. The noisy tin again sent the foxes out of their tree, and we listened carefully. Kitty thought she had heard faint quarrelling noises after she had chased them away for the last time on the previous day. It seemed as if the foxes were jockeying for position in another tree. Now we both heard them, but so faintly that it was impossible to decide their exact direction. Taking the binoculars I climbed the tree from which we had chased them. Once above the dense tangle of the jungle the squealing cries were more distinct, and a glance in that direction, even without the binoculars, gave the answer. Standing above the jungle was another tall tree very similar to the one in which they had made their camp. The binoculars told the whole story. There were many more flying-foxes in the other tree than had camped in this tree. There had been two camps, and when it got noisy in this one, the flying-foxes had gone over to the neighbours for the day.

I reported the situation to Kitty. She peered up at me rather hopelessly. "I've done some queer things for films," she said, "but I simply can't be in two places at once."

"No need for that. I know how we can fix it," I called back, and started to climb down.

Back at the camp I took the sheets from my bed, cut two long saplings, and fastened the sheets to the poles; then, taking a coil of rope, I hastened back. Soon the two sheets on their flagpoles were streaming out and flapping loudly in the steady trade-wind. There was no chance of the flying-foxes returning to this camp while those sheets flapped above the tree.

Before descending the tree I used the binoculars to search for the best approach to this other flying-fox camp. We both wore a criss-crossed pattern of scratches from the thorny wait-a-while vines, and the thought of pushing our way for an added quarter of a mile through the dense undergrowth was not a happy one. The new camp was only about two or three hundred yards in from the beach. Our best plan would be to make our way out on to the beach and walk round the island in the open. There were two big "nigger-heads", great blocks of coral several tons in weight that had been torn from their beds on the ocean floor and tossed up on the reef edge by a cyclone. These made good markers. If we turned back into the bush about a hundred yards past them we should find the flying-foxes.

We had no trouble in reaching them. One camera was soon in position, and I was ready to depart for my "hide" in the coral-tree.

"I'd better give you half an hour this time before I commence my tin-can concerto," said Kitty.

I thought for a moment. "Twenty minutes should still be about right." I shouldered the other camera and tripod. "No more jungle for me, I'm going to walk round the beach to the coral-tree."

I was just completing the setting up of the camera when faintly I heard a noble tattoo on the tin. From my tree it looked as if a factory chimney was belching a cloud of black smoke into the sky. The cloud spread out, then, forming into a long line, made straight for the old camp. Just before reaching the streaming, flapping bed-sheets it swerved abruptly and split up into a great mass of whirling molecules which again came together in a dark cloud and returned in the direction from whence they had come. The cloud shrank and got more dense as it descended towards their tree, reminding me of the Arabian nights, and how the genie must have looked going back into his bottle. Kitty, with her tin, was giving a magnificent performance. Up went the flying-foxes again. Time after time they tried to return, but that banging tin drove them away. The whirling cloud spread out wider and wider until it had broken up into hundreds of individual flying-foxes whirling wide over the tree-tops. The outer edge of the whirling circle approached. High above the coral-tree they flew; I could see their heads turning from side to side, and their beady eyes searching the scene beneath them. Would they decide to descend and land in the coral-tree? Perhaps the huge blossoms held no attraction during the day. What would they know of the brilliant red of the flowers when the only previous acquaintance had been during the dark of the night. This tree, so brilliant in its floral decoration that it seemed ready to burst into crackling flames, might frighten them away until night subdued its glory into a mere banquet table for diners who preferred subdued lighting.

Parting the leaves on the side where the sun was shining showed me that I could hope for no more than one more hour of sunshine. Anxiously I returned to my peep-hole in the roof. The foxes were circling lower, and all seemed to be eyeing the coral-tree as the principal target. There was subdued sloosh-sloosh-sloosh, and the rustle of twigs rubbing together. Quickly I parted the leaves and saw a flying-fox hanging head down, wings half extended as if ready for immediate flight, and sharp eyes glaring suspiciously around. Another, and yet another fox landed near it. For a few moments they held heated converse, with much baring of their gleaming teeth. But why should they be so annoyed? If they would only look at things philosophically the unusual happenings need result in no more than an early breakfast. The shrill chattering died down, only to burst forth again as more foxes landed in the tree. Why all this pointless discussion! There was left barely half an hour of sunlight. Again the chattering subsided, and the foxes festooned the tree in wary silence. Now perhaps they would eat. One after another they wrapped their wings around themselves—and went to sleep! Despairingly I peeped out at the motionless animals; fifteen minutes and the sun would set, and then whatever they did would be beyond the power of my camera to record.

A late comer landed amid a group of sleeping foxes, and demanded *Lebensraum* by shoving and snarling at its neighbours. There was a general reshuffle of bough positions, and again preparation for sleep. The flying-fox nearest the end of the bough sidled a little farther along to get farther from its neighbours. Alongside it was a huge bunch of coral flowers. In the very act of wrapping its wings around its body it paused, stretched out a pointed quivering nose towards the blossoms, sniffed, then reaching out with its grappling hook "thumb", swung into the mass of flowers. My camera was purring softly. Now—would it eat the petals? There was a flash of sharp little teeth, and a few petals fell to the ground uneaten and unwanted. The sharp little muzzle was pushed deep into the heart of the flower laid bare by the biting off of the discarded petals. Nectar, not blossoms was what the flying-foxes sought. These were not gluttons satisfied to gorge on the huge flamboyant blossoms, but gourmets with a nice discrimination and an appreciation of the sweet things in life. At it licked up the last of the nectar from each flower, the flying-fox would hang head downwards from the bough for a few seconds, and out would dart a long, slender pink tongue that carefully licked off the droplets of nectar adhering to the furry muzzle. Swinging to another flower, again only a few petals would be nipped off to open the way to the nectar-laden heart of the flower. "Fruit and nectar-eating bats" would seem to be the more accurate description of these quaint little flying mammals. I have no doubt that if the flower is small there is no punctilious discarding of petals; the whole flower would make but a tiny mouthful, and the scanty petals would not unduly distract from the sweetness of the nectar. Nevertheless, nectar is the main attraction.

Kitty was sitting out on the beach as I approached the deserted flying-fox camp. Before we were in hailing distance I performed a spirited little war dance concluding with a series of "V" signs. Kitty replied with the clasped-hands-above-the-head greeting of the success-ful pugilist. Beside her was an extraordinarily battered and misshapen object that had once been a kerosene-tin

"Did you get the deep blue background—golden manes agleam in the sun—borne aloft flame-like blossoms etc.?" said Kitty.

"All in the box, madame," I replied, with a courteous bow.

"Then, when we get back to camp, you may have a rum from the bottle I hid from you and the doctor." She picked up the shape-less tin and tossed it contemptuously back into the bushes. "Thank goodness I haven't got to perform on that thing again."

Good musicians should not have to perform on mediocre instruments.

CHAPTER 14

SEDUCTION IN THE SUN

E ARLY next morning I was round at the flying-fox camp to retrieve
my bed-sheets. As I unfastened the ropes holding up the white flags
that had helped to give us a victory, I saw, suspended from guy ropes
between the tree I was in and another some yards away, an enormous
spider-web. It was unbelievably beautiful, spangled with dew drops
and as large as a cart-wheel, with strands of a rich golden silk inter-
spersed with contrasting ribs of silver webbing. In the centre rested
a huge spider, which also had claims to beauty. The long legs were
coloured in alternate bands of bright yellow and very dark brown, and
the purplish body had a delicate silvery tracery of velvety hairs, while
the head was graced with a low conning tower whereon several
brilliantly gleaming eyes sparkled like the diamonds in a tiara. An
imposing lady, indeed, with her eight gaudy legs spread out in a
circle of at least six inches in diameter. This maker of golden nets is
Nephila, a most remarkable creature, with certain characteristics and
habits that are almost unique in the spider world.

The position of the web was most advantageous to its builder,
being placed directly across an aerial pathway between tall trees with
the tops of the lower trees only a few feet beneath. Any flying insect
breaking free of the confinement of the dense undergrowth would
almost certainly speed up on what would seem a main thoroughfare
for the aerial-minded, and drive at full speed into the net.

She was a good subject for filming, but in a rather difficult position for the placement of the camera. The best viewpoint from the
tree I was occupying was not close enough for a good picture of such a
relatively small subject; and the trees on the other side of the narrow
passage looked equally unsatisfactory. While untying the sheets from
the saplings, I had an idea. Placing the butt of one sapling in an adjacent
crotch in the tree, I allowed the other end to fall towards a tree across the
passage-way. With the other sapling allowed to fall at an angle into
another crotch, I had the rudiments of a bridgeway across the chasm.

127

Now if I was out in the centre of those two saplings, such a camera position should be ideal. Of course these two saplings were much too flimsy for a foundation, but there was no shortage of suitable material in the bush around me.

Back at the camp I collected cameras, ropes, boards from a packing-case, hammer and nails, and, with Kitty carrying the axe, was soon back at the tree. Two suitable young trees were felled and trimmed, and I climbed up into the tree with the ropes. I dropped an end of the rope to Kitty, who fastened it to the poles, which were then dragged laboriously up into the tree. A most unexpectedly exasperating task that was, for the heavy poles kept swinging in circles, and seemed to choose to get into positions where they would jam fast among the branches. I would have to tie my end of the rope to a bough, clamber down to the poles, free them, climb back, and commence hauling again—until the next jam. Finally they were placed with one end in the crotch of the tree; and with a guiding rope running from a stout bough above me, the poles swung across the gulf, and the bridge was becoming a reality. Again the rope was dropped to Kitty, who sent me up the boards, hammer, and nails, and I worked my way along the poles building my bridge before me.

The bridge completed, I took the camera out to the centre and delightedly set it up in a perfect position from which to photograph the spider and its web. But what a shock when I lined up the camera! I would get the spider in nice sharp focus, and the next second it was just a fuzzy blur. The wind was catching the tops of the tall tree and the branches were in continuous motion. I lowered the rope for the axe and chopped off the tops of the two branches that formed the crotch from which I had commenced to build the bridge. With all that top hamper cut away there should be much less swaying. There was—but still too much for a perfect picture. I had started so blithely on this idea, but it was rapidly developing into a very difficult problem. I sat on a bough and thought it over. Guy ropes running from the bridge to the trunks of adjacent trees should stop the movement. But wait—why stop the movement? To do that would require a regular maze of diverging ropes, and much climbing of the trees to which the ropes would have to be fastened. The real trouble was not the movement: it was the fact that the movement of the bough to which the spider's web was fastened and the movement of my bridge did not synchronize. That could soon be tested. A rope from each end of the bridge was fastened to the bough from which the spider's web was suspended. Anxiously I watched through the camera; certainly we were still swaying, but swaying in unison, and the camera remained in perfect focus. Gleefully I called to Kitty that everything was satisfactory. Her face looked worried as she gazed up at me.

"Are you sure that bridge thing is safe? It doesn't look it."

It might not look strong, but I had no doubt it would support a much greater weight than would be required.

Kitty was not easily reassured, and concluded with the ominous remark, "You know how you are liable to forget everything else when you are filming. Well, I'm telling you now," she paused, then very deliberately, "if you fall, I'll never speak to you again."

Looking down at her anxious face I realized that she had meant that last remark to be ambiguous. Some years before I had been working on the top of a high tower, and just glanced away from my camera to see a fellow cameraman alongside me in the act of stepping back from his camera—into space. I made a desperate grab for him, and for a few seconds we both teetered on the edge of the drop. A moment of absentmindedness can prove fatal. I climbed up to the stout bough above the bridge and fastened a rope to the bough; back again on the bridge, I tied a loop of the rope around me. Now I could be careless, or my bridge could break, and I would be merely suspended like a spider from the end of its web. If necessary I could climb back into the tree by climbing up the rope. Kitty gave a satisfied smile, waved her hand in farewell, and departed to continue with her camp chores.

Nephila, unlike most spiders, spins her snare in two colours. The spokes of the huge wheel are of a strong, dry, silvery silk that has less elasticity than the usual spider web. This is the rigid foundation for the closely wound golden spiral, a thick, wet silk, coated with an extraordinarily tenacious adhesive. Put your finger against one of these golden strands and press: it stretches like a piece of elastic, and as you draw your finger away the sticky web stretches to an amazing degree before either breaking from the web, or reluctantly pulling free to snap back rather loosely into its former position.

The organs from which the silken web is produced are a marvel of design. Inside the abdomen of the spider are specialized glands that secrete a liquid silk. Tubes extend from these glands, of which there are a number, to the spinnerets, the amazingly efficient loom, where the changing of the fluid into silk thread is accomplished by contact with the air. Here also a great number of minute tenuous threads are woven into the single strong fabric with which the spider-web is built. It is as if the spider plaited a silken rope from water.

A microscope is required to examine the intricacies of this beautifully designed mechanism. Beneath the lens, no longer do we see a ragged tuft of stubby hairs, but batteries of neat little nozzles like those on fire-brigade hoses, or, a comparison nearer to home, those little gadgets used to put decorative icing on cakes. The fluid has flowed from the internal glands down the tiny pipelines in the spider's interior, and has reached the nozzles, but it does not just gush at random from each little nozzle. The internal glands manufacture silks with differing characteristics, and these must be blended by the spinnerets in order to manufacture silks suitable for the particular purpose for which they are to be used. Each little nozzle is in perfect control, not only of the flow, but of the direction of the flow. The tiny nozzles flicker back and forth into position, flow is stopped in some nozzles, speeded up in others, while continuously the loom gives forth its silken thread. The production capacity of that miniature loom is far beyond expectation. A spider was coaxed to fasten the beginning of her thread to a spindle which was wound up as the silk was produced. When her supply of silk was exhausted she had spun an unbroken thread of three hundred yards in length! Women have worn silken gloves and hosiery that have been manufactured from the silk woven by the spider's tiny looms. Only the cheapness of green fodder for silkworms as compared to the difficulty of supplying spiders with their meaty meals has prevented the spider from being a provider of pure silk.

Nephila had selected a most rewarding place to spread her net. As I watch, a big tree-cricket leaps into the meshes, setting the whole web aquiver. In a flash *Nephila* has darted from the centre of the web, and from a few inches distance observes the struggles of her captive. This can be a dangerous encounter unless caution prevails. The formidable jaws of the cricket can give a bite that will bring blood from a human hand. Its great head is immobolized in the sticky web, but not so the powerful hind-legs with rows of armoured spikes like deadly spear-points at the ready. Cautiously *Nephila* creeps forward, then in a graceful arch one of her long forelegs is poised above the captive. Like the crack of a whip that foreleg slaps the cricket's face! What sort of behaviour is this! What a lady! Talk about adding insult to injury! No wonder the cricket's powerful hind-legs are lashing out in a fury of indignation. *Nephila* watches unmoved. She sidles a short distance round the cricket before again extending her foreleg. Surely she will not repeat her vulgar action! Again that flashing slap. Again the hind-legs lash out in impotent fury. *Nephila* sidles yet farther round her writhing victim. Once more the slap. Once more the kicking. Slowly the kicking subsides, then like a flash *Nephila* darts in, and with one lightning stroke of her powerful mandibles shears one of the formidable hind-legs clean off at the top joint. The severed leg is still falling towards the ground beneath as *Nephila* takes up her position on the opposite side of the cricket, and commences to repeat her slapping tactics. At last I realize the necessity for the apparently sadistic treatment of her prey. That irritating slap is necessary in order that *Nephila* may know just how wide an area is covered by that furious kicking. To go within it would be instant death. Once that fatal area is known a safe path may be chosen, and the menacing leg quickly amputated. The leg safely out of the way, her needle-sharp mandibles speedily inject the venom from the poison sacs at their base, and a numbness seeps through the struggling cricket bringing a speedy end to its struggles, and a quiet death.

Nephila has none of the unpleasant ways of a cat playing with a doomed mouse: her actions are those of sound common sense. According to an ancient Greek legend, Pallas Athene, the Goddess of Wisdom, turned a human maid into a spider as a punishment for her overweening conceit. Maybe that unfortunate maid was an ancestor of *Nephila*, for the wise Pallas Athene would surely have been generous enough to add a little of her own bountiful gift of wisdom as a partial recompense for the severity of the punishment. The name of that poor girl of ancient Greece was Arachne, hence the scientific name given to all the spider family—Arachnida.

Nephila, you are not a graceless virago. One raking kick of the cricket's powerful spiked legs on your soft and unprotected abdomen would mean certain disembowelment; and how would the cricket benefit from the delivery of a death blow to her captor? Though the torn body of *Nephila* might fall in dying agony to the earth below, the cricket would remain to grow weaker and weaker in the sticky meshes of the web until a long-delayed death stilled its futile struggles.

One morning as I approached the tree to climb on to my bridge to continue filming the daily doings of *Nephila*, I disturbed a number of silver-eyes, small green birds that are very numerous in the island bush. One of the silver-eyes sped in startled flight directly along the aerial pathway towards the golden web. So swift was its flight that I expected it to hurtle like a bullet through the web. It saw the web too late, attempted to dodge, but flew at full speed into the snare. The web bellied out in a huge bulge where the bird struck, but immediately snapped back into shape again with the silver-eye held fast to the sticky threads. With all speed I got the camera in position, expecting to record an instance of how a spider sets free a creature so powerful that, before it could be subdued, it would destroy the web.

Nephila was already circling the captive, and, as I saw the frantically fluttering wings break some of the web strands, I prepared to get a film of *Nephila* hurriedly cutting away the remaining strands to free such a destructive captive. But no! As I focus the camera on her she moves across to windward and turns her back towards the fluttering bird, then her great paunch lifts high away from the net. As I watch, the spinnerets send forth a shimmering mist of the finest gossamer, which streams out in the wind towards the struggling bird. No longer does her silk loom plait the threads into a rope. Each tiny nozzle streams out its thin thread parallel to that of each neighbouring nozzle. The threads travel down wind and, like a shower from the rose of a fairy watering can, the mist sinks towards the beating wings, which break it into infinitesimal particles.

How can *Nephila* expect to use such fragile cords to subdue so lusty and muscular an opponent? It is a gallant attempt, but failure is surely inevitable. Cut free the bird, *Nephila*, or be reconciled to building a new web to replace what will soon be a hopeless wreck. *Nephila*, the mist-maker stands firm. Out floats the mist without a pause, and now the green wings are disappearing in a fog. Each frantic wing-stroke gathers more silk: soft and subtle stuff, clinging close, clogging the force of every wing beat, clinging between body and wing as the weakening bird struggles to lift its wing away from its sticky fog-shrouded side. Slower and slower are the wing-beats, thicker grows the intangible fog. Then *Nephila* raises her two hind-legs, gathers the filmy mist into tiny bundles of fairy-floss, and tosses them on to the feebly struggling bird. Where they fall, they cling. Mounting up, they muffle all movement. Motionless now, the bird lies in a silken shroud like one already dead. The spinnerets cease their mist-making. *Nephila* wheels, and sinks her poison fangs deep into the neck close to the base of the bird's skull. And so she remains as the sun passes behind the trees to leave the web in sombre shadow.

The wooing of *Nephila* is the strangest episode I have witnessed in the love life of any creature. I had noticed what I thought was a little red mite wandering over the leaves near the supporting strands of the web, but had paid it scant attention. This day it climbed down one of the web supports and began moving cautiously about the outer edges of the web. I looked at it more closely. It was a very minute male spider. Several times it came towards *Nephila*, who completely disregarded it until a mis-step apparently caused a signal to tremble along the strands of her web. Immediately she turned towards the tiny spider; but the web was again still, for the little male remained motionless. Again the stealthy approach, but this time *Nephila* saw the intruder, and started along the web in pursuit. The little fellow showed an amazing turn of speed despite his small size. *Nephila* was at least one thousand times greater in bulk, but he was an elusive sprinter and could dodge like a first-grade footballer. As she returned to the centre of her web, the little spider followed her cautiously. She had barely settled down again when, driven by an overpowering passion for this imposing giantess, the little fellow with a flashing burst of speed raced towards her, jumped on to one of her massive hind-legs, climbed up it like a monkey on a pole, and landed on her great, broad back. There he clung as if regaining breath. One could imagine a "Phew!—that was a close go!" A juicy cicada flew into the web, and *Nephila* apparently forgot about her Lilliputian lover; her thoughts were strictly on business. As she moved about the web attending to the preparation of her meal, the little spider rode round perched on her back where he looked ridiculously like a skinny little pygmy mahout on an outsize elephant. As *Nephila* settled down to her meal, he wandered about on her immense back as if enjoying the view from the flat roof of a city sky-scraper. Peering over the edge he looked down her immense side with all the absorbed interest of a true rubberneck watching the traffic in the streets far below. *Nephila* was in the middle of dinner when the absurd little male decided that, for love, this was as good a time as any. He was over the edge and racing down her side and underneath her great abdomen in a wild rush. *Nephila* reared up in rage at such an unwarranted and untimely attempt on her virtue. Standing high above her web she raked her great legs backwards and forwards along her body. He narrowly escaped annihilation, but dodged under one massive leg and swung himself on to another as it swept towards him, raced up the leg, made a neatly executed leap, and was once more perched on her back. *Nephila* went back to her dinner.

This happened several times as again and yet again his consuming passion overcame his discretion. The outrageous difference in dimensions makes such a love affair appear too ridiculous to be true; but so it is between the *Nephila* maid and her swain. Perhaps this is the reason why love seems to hold no interest for the lady. It seems that her diminutive lover must rape her by stealth if she is ever to become a mother.

Another opportunity came as she was drowsily resting after her cicada meal. Stealthily he crept down, and, with a few quick dabs of his sperm-laden palpi, made *Nephila* an expectant mother. Only as, the deed accomplished, he was scampering across the web, did *Nephila* seem to realize the enormity of the outrage for which he was responsible. Like a flash she raced after him, he dodged this way, that way—the stealthily seduced *Nephila* would not be baulked. A snap of her great mandibles and he was transfixed. He must have been no more than a pinch of meat to *Nephila*, but perhaps she regarded him as a minute steak, with vengeance sauce.

Yet, is it fair to regard his death so flippantly? For the love of a lady he died. Consider other lovers who have had their exploits proclaimed by minstrels down the ages. Which of these fathered more than eight hundred offspring? He did. I know. When they arrived I counted *Nephila's* babies.

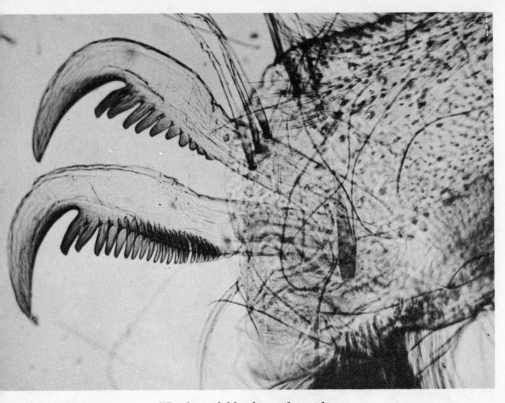

The formidable claws of a spider.

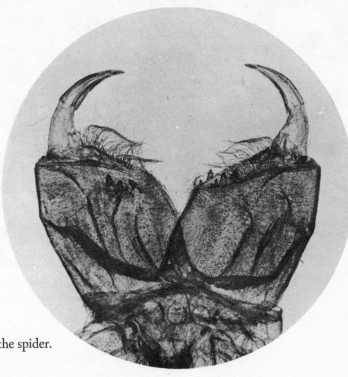

The deadly poison fangs of the spider.

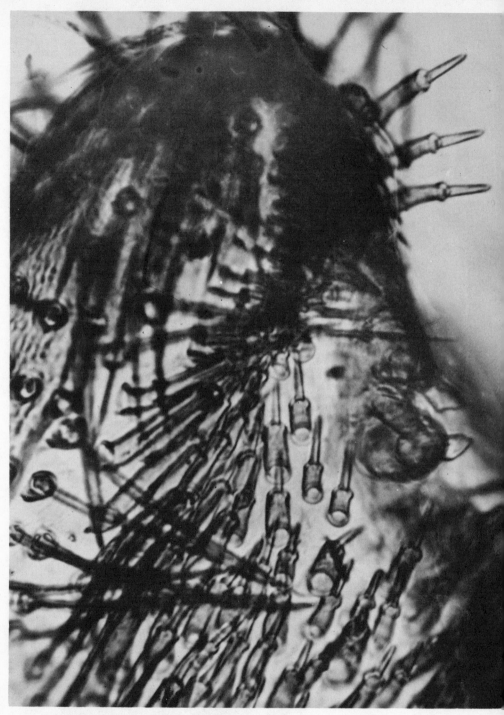

The loom of the spider (spinnerets). Liquid streaming through the tiny nozzles is woven into the silk of the spider's web. (Greatly magnified.)

CHAPTER 15

WE GET THE BIRD

IT has been said that while it is not necessary to be mad to make motion pictures, it certainly helps. At times, when my patience has been sorely tried, I have ruefully decided that there is some truth in this. But the work is so fascinating, there is such a feeling of triumph when you know a good scene is safely in the box, that one keeps on keeping on.

Having found the creatures to be filmed, one's troubles are only beginning. Wild life does not take kindly to being photographed, and ways and means must be found to obtain your pictures without the shy creatures becoming aware of the camera. With the "still" camera, the photographing of wild animals is not so difficult. Often a photograph is required illustrating only one particular phase of the creature's life; and if the creature lives where the light is dim, the aid of a flashlight will secure the photo without much trouble. But in most cases artificial light is ruled out for motion pictures of wild animals, because one is seeking not an isolated snapshot, but a complete record of the habits and life history.

When shy birds are to be filmed, it is necessary to build a small house of branches and leaves in the trees where the birds make their nests. While the birds are away seeking nest-building materials, one climbs into this "hide". In the leafy wall, a small opening is made to allow the camera to be focused on the nest. Although the hours spent within the hide may often be long, they need not necessarily be monotonous. Often while waiting to obtain my bird pictures, I have observed unexpected comedies and dramas being enacted by the other wild inhabitants of the forest.

On one such occasion I heard a rustling behind me in the leaves of the hide. Glancing back over my shoulder, I saw a large snake glide through the hide and down the tree on to the ground. At first I thought that some movement of mine had disturbed it, then in a small clearing I saw what was interesting the snake. It was a large male bush-rat.

These rodents are no slinking searchers after refuse, but big lithe jungle hunters, with more than a fair share of courage and aggressiveness. The rat, unaware of the proximity of the snake, was contentedly nibbling at some morsel of food. The snake glided into the clearing. Sensing its approach, the rat abruptly lifted its head and stood stock still gazing at the snake. The snake returned the gaze for a moment or two, then commenced to glide forward. When two or three feet away from the rat it stopped and raised its head from the ground, at the same time curving its neck into a graceful S-curve preparatory to striking. For quite three minutes not a move was made by either of the adversaries. So still were they that one could imagine that each had been frozen stiff by the cold glare of its enemy. Then without warning the rat left the ground as if thrown into the air. To my amazement, it was not attempting to escape, but had made a tremendous bound on to the snake and was biting deep into its body. With a furious hiss, the snake struck at the rat, but its head merely hit the ground where the rat had been a fraction of a second before. The rat was now biting savagely into another gleaming coil. In a fury, the snake struck again; nothing could have evaded that flashing stroke, so swift was the motion that it was merely a blur. As it bit into the body of the rat, it simultaneously threw a loop around the rat and commenced to tighten upon it. The rat gave a startled squeak as the breath was forced from its body, for this was not a venomous snake, but a python, which kills its prey by squeezing it to death. The rat was not yet subdued. Wriggling like an eel, it slipped its body out of the strangling coil, but it could not escape. It was almost impossible to follow the rapid movements of the snake's body as loop after loop was flung unerringly round the rat, which struggled desperately, fiercely kicking at the snake with its hind-legs and tearing at the scaly body with its front paws, while it never ceased to bite furiously into the coils that were strangling it; but despite its frenzied struggles it could not free itself. One final coil lashed round the throat of the rat, and then commenced a relentless tightening of all the coils. A rhythmic pulsation could be seen flowing along the body of the snake, the only outward sign of the tremendous pressure that was being brought to bear upon the hapless victim. For a few moments the rat struggled desperately, then suddenly—all was still. It was only then that I realized that automatically I had swung the camera into position and had secured a complete motion picture record of the event. That unexpected film was to prove more interesting to the public than the film of the birds that took so much more trouble and time to secure.

A hollow tree can sometimes be used as a hide, but on one occasion it was not so successful. Scrub-fowl were making a nest mound in the dense bush near the centre of the island. The nest of the scrub-fowl is a communal affair; several of the hens combine forces, and by scratching the leaves amongst the undergrowth together they heap them up into a large mound many feet in diameter and two or three feet high. The hens scratch a hole in the mound and lay their eggs, then more leaves are raked together and the eggs carefully covered up, the mound steadily growing in height as the busy mothers build the leafy cradles. The scrub-fowl does not sit on her eggs to incubate them; the warmth generated in the heap of rotting vegetation does the job for her. The chicks hatch out and scratch their way up through the nest, able to take care of themselves from the time they break out of the shells.

Since the birds usually start work on their mound at dawn, I made my way in the darkness through the jungle to the hollow tree, set the motion picture camera up, and waited patiently for the actresses to appear on the set. Keen and alert, I gazed out through a peephole cut in the side of the tree. The sunlight was just beginning to filter down into the jungle, and at any minute the birds should come wandering through the undergrowth to continue working on the mound. Ah! Here they come! Softly the camera starts to whir, and to my delight some of the birds commence work, raking up the leaves and adding them to the mound, whilst others are scratching holes preparatory to laying their eggs. The noise of the camera is completely muffled inside that helpful old tree. My cramped limbs are forgotten as I happily crank the camera.

But what is that itchy, stinging heat spreading over my body? Despite my intense desire to scratch, I keep the camera turning. Something drops on the back of my neck and begins an exploration. Hell! It becomes too inquisitive! I grit my teeth and try to ignore the indignity, but the searching inquiry into my person becomes absolutely unendurable. I make a frenzied grab at the impudent intruder, and

137

receive a vicious bite from a big centipede. With a yell of pain and anger I burst out of the hollow tree. The startled scrub-fowl flee in panic, leaving me to treat my centipede bite, and to dig a hundred or so scrub itch mites out of my skin into which they are burrowing industriously, pleased to be out of dead wood and into living me.

I spent the rest of the day in fumigating and smoking out the hollow tree, and was back again next morning before dawn, but bad weather set in, making the light too dim for motion picture photography. I spent weeks in the hide in the vain hope that the sun might break through the clouds and filter down into the depths of the forest, but the bad weather continued and I never completed the film. One day, under a leaden sky, I had the melancholy pleasure of seeing the chicks scratch their way out of the nest and scamper away into the under-growth.

A good light is always a doubtful hope in wild life photography, so when starting out to film *Birds of the Barrier Reef* I prepared for emergencies by taking an electric light plant with me.

The first island we visited was lonely Nor' West Island in the Capricorn Group. It is a tiny coral island barely three miles in circum-ference, uninhabited apart from nesting sea birds, sand crabs, cock-roaches, centipedes and spiders, and turtles in the mating season.

On a day of dazzling blue sky and sea, our boat sailed through the entrance and into the lagoon, and we dropped anchor close to a snow-white strip of beach. Leaving the crew to unload the equipment, Kitty went ashore with me to look over this uninhabited coral island. Un-inhabited, did I say? I had been told that nobody lived on this island, and yet there were well-trodden paths running in all directions from the top of the beach back into the bush. Was the island enchanted and were fairies in residence, or had a tribe of pygmies settled here? The trees grew so low above the much-used paths that to move along them it was necessary to crawl on hands and knees. We had travelled about fifty yards in this way when suddenly the ground gave way beneath me, and the next second, spitting out a mouthful of sand, I clambered out of a mutton bird burrow; the indignant householder, taking advantage of my downfall, carried out a successful flank attack with its sharp, hooked beak. I had no sooner stepped out of that burrow than down I went into another, accompanied by shrieks of unfeeling laughter from Kitty, who was following close behind.

"Oh, you do look funny," she giggled.

With dignity I turned to her. "My good woman——" I said. There was a cloud of dust and a squeal.

"Stop good-womaning me and help me out of here," she spluttered from the depths of a mutton bird burrow.

"Certainly, my dear; but I was only going to say when you so rudely interrupted, that it might be interesting to go more deeply into this matter of mutton bird burrows."

Investigation showed that the soft sandy soil was riddled with the burrows. The mutton birds were nesting there in hordes, and from all around us came wails and groans as if souls in torment were buried beneath us. Of all the birds I know, I think the mutton bird makes the most hideous noises. It wails like a lost child, groans like a man *in extremis*, screeches like a railway whistle, and emits bubbling gurgles like a drowning man going down for the third time. And all this is supposed to express the undying love a mutton bird bears for its mate! A veritable Johnny Ray of the birds!

Later we pegged out an area of the island and counted the number of burrows within that area, multiplying that figure by the approximate total area used as nesting space. Making no allowance for chicks, there must have been three or four million mutton birds nesting on that one tiny island.

This, however, was not the entire avian population. The pisonia-trees above us were laden with the nests of the white-capped noddies, so much so that each bird was almost within pecking range of its neighbour. Later calculations gave us the huge total of five or six million noddies nesting in the trees! Dainty little birds are the noddies, slightly built and about the size of a dove, dull black in colour, with a neat white cap on the head. Upon very short acquaintance they became so friendly that they would even allow us to stroke them while they sat on their nests. Hides were quite unnecessary when filming them, for they had no fear of the camera.

The nesting season brings a miserable death to many of the noddies. The pisonia-trees in which they build their nests possess very sticky seeds. Unfortunately, the nesting season of the noddies coincides with the falling of twigs loaded with the seeds from the pisonia-trees, and the ground becomes thinly carpeted with the seeds. The noddies, searching the ground for dead pisonia-leaves with which to build their crude platform-like nests, often get a twig of these sticky seeds adhering to their feathers. The birds attempt to pull these seeds off with their beaks, but the seeds cling tenanciously to their plumage. If the noddies fly up into the trees and manage to pick the seeds free, everything is all right; but often the birds struggle to get them off whilst remaining on the ground, and this spells disaster. While they are struggling with one twig, they come into contact with other twigs. Soon their feet and legs are matted with twigs and they trip when attempting to walk. When they fall to the ground, they struggle to their feet with bunches of the seeds hanging to their feathers. In desperation they try to fly, but their wings are almost bound to their bodies, and they crash back amongst the seeds, where they roll over and over, picking up more and more in their struggles, until they are just big balls of sticky seeds. Helplessly bound up in the centre of these balls, the poor noddies await a slow death.

When we first found them in this condition, my wife and I spent hours picking the seeds off and cleaning the feathers; but after finding hundreds of noddies in the same sad plight we realized the impossibility of continuing such a hopeless task. Until the nests were built, and the noddies no longer searched for leaves, we found no pleasure in strolling through the pisonia groves.

I am afraid that we never developed much love for the mutton birds; they seemed so stupid and clumsy. At dusk they returned to the island from their day's fishing, and often announced their arrival by knocking over the lamp on the dinner table. When the light was re-lit they would greet it with an idiotic chuckle, climb out of the stew or the butter, and make a shuffling run across the dinner table, tipping over everything they touched. Then they would sidle up to the teapot, ogling and crooning to it in the most heart-broken tones. The teapot paying no attention to this loving chatter, they would rush back across the table, attempt to fly—and knock the lamp over again. When lifted up and put outside, they almost invariably vomited smelly, partially digested fish over one's hands. I could never decide if this was a defensive or offensive action. Exasperating pests, the mutton birds.

They arrive at Nor' West Island for the nesting season about October, dig their burrows, lay and incubate their eggs, and then both parents feed the young with half-digested fish, which they regurgitate. So assiduously do the parent birds attend to the feeding of the young that within a comparatively short period the chicks are bigger than their parents, and bloated with fat. The parent birds now lose all interest in their young and leave the island. The young mutton birds are left in the burrows to exist on their accumulated fat, which lasts them for some weeks. During this period their feathers are developing into adult plumage instead of the soft down of the chick, and the young birds can be seen on the open beach trying out their wings. Very clumsy they are for the first few days: with wildly beating wings they run along the sand, take off, and fly erratically for a yard or two, then nose-dive into the sand. However, in a few weeks they are flying quite efficiently, and in little groups fly away from the island. When the mating urge comes to the young birds, they fly back to the islands where they were born, and in their turn bring forth a new generation of young mutton birds.

They are heavily built birds and have difficulty in getting into the air without a clear space in which to taxi along until they gain enough speed to take off. When returning from their fishing expeditions they land on the open beach and make their way on foot to their underground nests. This was the explanation of the well-trodden paths leading from the beach back into the bush; they were made by the feet of millions of birds going to and from their nests. Since several million birds leave the island every morning to go fishing, and are not able to gain flying speed among the trees, everything must be properly organized or there would be chaos. Before sunrise they leave their burrows and walk in a thickly packed mass along the paths to the top of the beach where, on the open sand, they are able to gather speed and become airborne.

I was anxious to obtain a moving picture of this early morning march of the mutton birds. Knowing that it would take place before daybreak, I had brought the electric light plant to the island. After nightfall, when the birds had retired to their burrows (but obviously not to sleep, for the caterwauling went on all night) we began work on one of the paths. Lanterns were lighted and hung in the trees, giving us a dim working light. The electric generator was set up along the beach, and the cables to carry the current were run along to the arc lamps, which were spaced at intervals along the pathway. The movie camera was set up and carefully focused. All was in readiness by the time the first faint glow of dawn began to warm the morning clouds.

A long drawn sigh stole out of the island bush and gathered in strength until it could be recognized as the sound of millions of birds' feet shuffling over the dead leaves. A musty, fishy odour wafted to our nostrils. Coming events were casting their scent before them; quite unforgettable is the smell of mutton birds in the mass. Then in the dim light of the lanterns we saw a weird spectacle. It looked as if a gigantic bottle of ink had been poured out on the ground and was running in streams towards the sea. A river of birds flowed down the path, shoulder to shoulder, ten abreast, the beaks of those behind touching the tails of those in front. It was an amazing sight! The island was literally carpeted with birds! On they flowed, with an occasional hold-up when an amorous swain tried to make love. But amongst the mutton birds, all the world does not love a lover, and after a moment-ary halt the lovers were swept indignantly aside, and the march continued.

This was the moment we had prepared for, and with a hiss and a splutter on went the arc lights. Immediately the pathway was as bright as day, and the camera went into action. The river of birds rushed towards me, then became a tidal wave. Camera, arc lamps, and camera-man were engulfed beneath a seething sea of claws, beaks, and beat-ing wings. The mutton birds must have thought they had all slept in, and the sun had stolen a march on them.

As I ruefully surveyed the overturned camera and lights, I made up my mind that from then on I would leave all mob scenes to Cecil B. de Mille.

CHAPTER 16

INVADED FROM THE SEA

THE day had been hot and oppressive. It was getting near to the monsoons, and the south-east trade-wind that tempered the tropical heat of our island was becoming weak and fitful. Night came like a warm curtain of black velvet. We were glad to climb under the mosquito nets and call it a day. The tent flaps were left wide open so any little breeze that came our way might stir the hot air. With the mutton birds' chorus for a lullaby, we drifted into sleep.

Crash! I saw stars! Something had struck me a savage glancing blow on the head. Struggling to get up from my camp stretcher I was suddenly tied up in the folds of mosquito net. The bed teetered back and forth for a second or two and then over it went. Kitty called out in fright as I rolled in the sand, and in my furious struggles I nearly overturned her bed. Then a smothering mass of canvas came down—the tent had collapsed! Slap! Thump! Sand began to bury us in the ruins. On and on the steady slapping and thumping went, while the weight of sand heaping up above me steadily increased. The feeling of being buried alive gave me a desperate strength, and I forced a hand through the strangling net and ripped it down. A few seconds later I had pulled Kitty clear of the ruins and we were free. But what had happened? Our electric torches were somewhere under the heap of canvas, which, from the sound, was still being buried beneath the sand.

We groped our way through the darkness to the camera and store tent and found another torch. As we neared our sleeping tent the torch showed showers of sand erupting from a big depression in the earth, and steadily piling up over our half-buried tent. Shining the torch into the depression showed a huge green turtle placidly digging her nest. She had come up from the sea and crawled straight through our open tent, carrying away the tent poles in her heedless progress.

There are three species of turtles that commonly nest on Barrier Reef islands; the hawksbill turtle, from which is obtained the valuable tortoiseshell; the loggerhead, which like the hawksbill is a fish-eater;

and the green turtle, a vegetarian, from whose flesh is made the famous turtle soup. Large numbers of the green turtles visit Nor' West Island every year to make their nests. They are huge creatures, averaging three or four hundredweight each. For all their great bulk and apparent clumsy build, they are swift swimmers, and with effortless strokes of their powerful flippers glide through the water as gracefully as birds fly in the air. But they leave all this airy grace behind them when they leave the water. As night descends, the caterwauling of the mutton birds is accompanied by a chorus of weary sighs from the turtles as they drag their ponderous bulk from the water and laboriously make their way up the beach to dig their nests. One cannot but feel sorry for the turtle when one sees her painful progression through the sand. No longer is her great bulk bouyed up by the sea; her four flippers must lift forward over the yielding sand nearly a fifth of a ton of turtle. Every few feet she rests and expels her breath in a deep sigh; her head sinks to the sand while great tears gather in her eyes. Despite her obvious discomfort and misery she sticks to her task with a weary patience. The number of painful steps she has taken from the sea to the top of the beach can be counted from the "dot and carry one" marks of her tail, as at the end of each lurching step forward she pauses and sinks back for a moment, driving her tail into the sand and making a little round hole. By these marks one is also able to tell whether the tracks were made by a turtle going up the beach to lay, or by one that has completed her nest, for she allows her tail to drag in the sand, cutting an unbroken furrow, when returning to the sea. A few hours after sunset the beach in the moonlight looks as if dozens of caterpillar tractors had been driven up out of the sea, so heavily imprinted in the sand are the tracks of the turtles.

Having reached the top of the beach, the turtle chooses an open patch of sand above high-water mark and clear of the roots of trees, and begins to make her nest. Happily she is not easily disturbed once she starts work, a fact that was of great assistance when the time came to set up the arc lights for filming. It is quite possible that the creature is half-blinded by the sand that clings to the mucus oozing from her eyes, and the light does not worry her; but a sudden noise is quite likely to cause her to cease her labours, and either look for another place to make a nest, or return to the sea.

With her front flippers she makes a depression in the sand about two yards across and a foot deep. The sand is not so much dug out as removed by powerful blows of the front flippers, which throw the sand out in showers as if being driven by miniature explosions. Then begins the digging of the egg pit, which is excavated by the hind flippers only, and an amazingly delicate piece of work it is. The great body slews slightly to the side and the flipper on one side is driven like a spade into the sand. But the sand is not shovelled out, it is lifted out. The end of the flat spade-like flipper curves like the fingers of a human hand, and the sand is carefully lifted, scarcely a grain being lost in the process. The great body slews again to one side, and the flipper on the other side repeats the process while, at the same moment, the sand held in the first flipper is thrown, with a quick jerk, well away from the nest. The delicate precision of the work is almost beyond belief; the turtle cannot see what she is doing, for she is working with her hind flippers, yet she digs in the yielding sand a nicely circular pit about nine inches in diameter and a foot or more deep. It is undoubtedly a work of sheer blind instinct, for I have seen turtles with only one hind flipper, the other having been lost most likely in an encounter with a shark, dig their nests quite obviously unaware of the fact that there was only one flipper to do the work. They would dig a flipperful of sand with one flipper, then the body would slew into position to allow the other flipper to be brought into use, whereupon the mangled stump would go through the useless motions of digging, lifting, and throwing away of sand with, of course, no effect. I have several times played proxy for the missing flipper in such a case, and the turtle and I have dug a nest together, she digging on one side, and I on the other. I must admit, however, that she made a better job of her side than I did of mine.

The pit being nicely dug, the egg laying commences. It is as well that the eggs have no limy shell; if they had they would certainly be broken as they fall into the egg pit; but they have a tough parchment-like skin, and if thrown on to the sand they bounce like a tennis ball. At first the eggs are laid slowly, about one a minute, but as the turtle warms to her task the tempo increases, and soon the eggs are tumbling rapidly into the pit. They are white, round, and slightly larger than a golf ball. The poultry farmer would be fortunate if it were possible to cross a turtle with a hen, for the turtle lays an average of 150 eggs at a sitting.

The eggs deposited in the pit, the turtle shovels the sand over them with her hind flippers, carefully filling up the hole and patting and packing the sand down until the eggs are completely covered. Then with the front flippers she scatters the sand about until all signs of the egg-pit are completely obliterated. Her maternal duties now at an end the turtle returns to the sea, completely washing her flippers of any further responsibility to her young.

The native crews of the bêche-de-mer and trochus luggers esteem the turtle eggs as a welcome addition to their diet. Their method of finding the nests is very simple, yet efficient. They search along the top of the beach until they find a spot which experience has taught them would be likely to be used by a turtle to make her nest. Driving spears into the sand, they probe the whole area until the spear is withdrawn with egg yolk adhering to it. At this spot the sand is scooped away, and the eggs collected. The yolk of the turtle egg is most palatable, but even with prolonged cooking the white will not set; it remains a slimy, unappetizing-looking jelly. We have often been forced to use turtle eggs when supplies have run short on isolated islands, and the yolks separated from the slimy whites have made us many good dishes.

When I first filmed the life of the turtle more than twenty-five years ago, all the scientific accounts I had read gave the incubation period of the turtle eggs as six weeks. I had carefully fenced in several nests after the turtles had returned to the sea, and on each fence had tied a label setting out the date of laying, for I wished to film the baby turtles emerging from the nest. At the expiration of six weeks we eagerly watched for the baby turtles, but none appeared. Seven weeks passed, and still no baby turtles. I began to wonder if the eggs in the marked nests were infertile, and decided to open a nest and have a look. The first egg opened relieved my mind; the egg was fertile and a little baby turtle lived within, but a large yolk sac was still attached to it, so the baby was not ready as yet to emerge from the egg. Eight weeks passed, and still no baby turtles! Was it possible that they were hatching, but escaping through my carefully built fences? These weeks of patient waiting on a lonely island must not be fruitless, so I decided to institute a turtle patrol. Kitty took it in turns with me to visit the nests day and night; four hours on, and four hours off, were our watches.

One day, almost incoherent with excitement, Kitty arrived back at the camp—the baby turtles were emerging from one of the nests! From the label tied to the fence around it, nine weeks and two days had elapsed since the turtle had deposited her eggs in that nest. The tiny turtles fairly poured up out of the sand. They were barely two inches across, but, unlike their lethargic parents, were brimming over with energy. No sooner had they reached the light and air, than they swung unerringly towards the sea, setting off at a great pace down the beach. They have no doubt about which direction the sea lies. Pick them up and turn them in whatever direction you wish: the moment they are placed back on the sand they swing in the right direction and scramble seawards. At first I thought that they must be guided by the slope of the beach towards the water, but this was not so. We placed some of them at the foot of a small sandhill at the top of the beach. From this position the little turtles had to climb upwards before they could reach the beach sloping down to the sea. But this did not confuse them; they immediately scaled the heights and made their way towards the sea.

For several days there had been an unwonted activity amongst the sea birds, which had kept up a steady day and night patrol of the beach surrounding the island. A passing silver gull sighted the young turtles making for the sea, and with a harsh cry swooped down at the scurrying youngsters. At that cry sea birds seemed to materialize from everywhere, and immediately the beach was a scene of horrible carnage as the sea birds squabbled over the torn and bleeding baby turtles. Shouting angrily, we ran down the beach to chase the screaming birds from their prey, but the sand was already strewn with the dead and dying. The few babies that had escaped made their way quickly to the water, and swam bravely towards the outer reef. They had only gone a short distance before the fish were amongst them, and again we witnessed a scene of pitiless slaughter. No wonder the turtle lays so many eggs; if it were not for this the species would have become extinct long ago with such heavy infant mortality.

We felt that something had to be done to protect the youngsters, and, at the risk of upsetting the balance of nature, we collected all the baby turtles as they emerged from the sand and set them free near the outer edge of the reef, where they would certainly escape the attacks of the birds waiting for them on the beach, and should have a better chance of escaping the hungry fish.

Since the adult green turtles are strict vegetarians, we were very surprised to discover that a few baby turtles we had kept as pets showed no interest in any sea plants we tried to feed them with, but greedily fought each other for small pieces of fish dropped into their tank. When two turtles grabbed opposite ends of the one portion, they would quickly snap it up until they arrived face to face, then each would eye its fellow with a long look of pained disgust. Suddenly one would try to take advantage of the other and, clamping its jaws firmly on the coveted piece of fish, would make a violent attempt to swim away with it. If it happened to be a tough piece of fish, a desperate tug-of-war would commence and continue until either the fish broke in half or one of the contestants had to relinquish its hold and swim to the surface for a fresh supply of air. Turtles are not fish, but must breathe air like land animals. A quick gulp of air, and down the little turtle would dive to see if it could grab the fish again before all had disappeared down its opponent's throat.

When we finally set our pet turtles free in the lagoon, they had grown to about the size of a saucer. One very rarely sees the intermediate stage of their growth. It is usual to see only the babies, each weighing merely a few ounces, and the full-grown adults weighing hundreds of pounds. How they spend the intermediate period of their growth is somewhat of a mystery.

CHAPTER 17

PIGS, PASTEUR, AND THE VOLCANO

THE majority of visitors to Australia's Great Barrier Reef never see the Great Barrier Reef. Most of the islands that cater for tourist traffic are close to the mainland, and many are actually pieces of the mainland that, ages ago, were separated by the sea from the coast. Although many of these islands are very lovely, they are not coral islands.

Because of the constant tramping over and despoiling of the fringing reefs on these inhabited islands, we had made our headquarters on a tiny, true coral island. It was uninhabited, and seldom visited except by our supply boat once a fortnight.

It was only a few days since our boat had called, so we were surprised one morning to see a distant sail expanding up from the horizon.

It was a bêche-de-mer lugger, and the native crew came ashore for fresh water and coconuts.

I seized the opportunity to question the natives about any unusual creatures or places they may have seen in the vicinity. One native had been a great traveller and, among other things, told me of "a big fella hole" he had seen when crossing a mountain range on the mainland. He admitted that he had not examined it closely, since he feared it might be the home of some mountain devil.

I thought it might be the entrance to a system of limestone caves and, having a weakness for exploring caves, I decided that the next time our supply boat called, we would go across to the mainland to see this devil's lair. After we had seen this place in the mountains, I wanted to visit another island where we might find new subjects for the cameras.

We packed all the gear and, as soon as we sighted the supply boat, broke camp, and were ready to depart.

On reaching a small settlement on the mainland we set about securing some means of transport. The only vehicle available was an ancient Ford. The tires contained no such luxuries as inner tubes, being merely covers packed with straw. Where the straw peeped through the cracked covers, fencing wire was bound round keeping the tires and their contents firmly in position. One would never have picked this vehicle off a junk heap, but the trials that battered old relic cheerfully survived would have done credit to a Rolls Royce. It knocked, rattled, screeched, and boiled, but kept going. Beneath the load of camping gear, moving-picture cameras, food-supplies, rifles, and four dogs, not to mention the human freight, its springs groaned and flattened.

The folk at the settlement had informed us that the mountain ranges we had to cross were inhabited by herds of wild pigs, and there might be a good opportunity to film a wild-pig hunt on the way to this "big fella hole" in the mountain; hence the hunting dogs and rifles.

An enthusiastic lady journalist, a recent arrival from overseas, was anxious to gather material for a travel book she was writing, and pleaded to be allowed to go with us. She was warned that she would have to rough it, but she was so keen to join the expedition that we consented. She seemed to lose a little of her happy enthusiasm when she caught sight of Leaping Lena, as we had dubbed the ancient Ford. However, plucking up courage, she scrambled in amongst the dogs, and, with a clattering roar, Lena leapt off towards the mountains. There was no middle course with Lena, she was either standing stock still, or off to a flying start—a trait which we found very trying to our neck muscles.

A few miles out the track ceased, and we had to take to the bush. To protect the radiator, which was in danger of being pierced by sharp branches, we cut saplings and fastened them as a screen in front of the car. From then on we progressed like an army tank, picking our way where the smallest trees and bushes grew, and mowing them down before us. Lena snorted and cavorted like a war horse, but leapt gallantly at each new obstacle.

That night we made camp alongside a river, and fishing lines were soon in action. The fish bit ravenously, and before long were grilling on stripped green gum twigs. So good was supper that we decided to catch more fish for breakfast, and thereby hangs a sad tale.

We were sitting on the river bank in the moonlight and, while waiting for the fish to bite, I filled in the time by warning our journalist

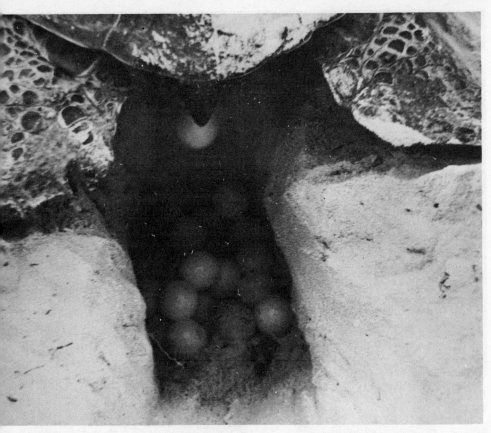

Soon the turtle eggs are tumbling rapidly into the pit.

A luminous marine worm. (Highly magnified; photo-micrograph
from the film *Secrets of the Sea.*)

Polyzoa, microscopic animals that live in colonies. Although they look like plants, each bud is a tiny marine animal. (Greatly magnified.)

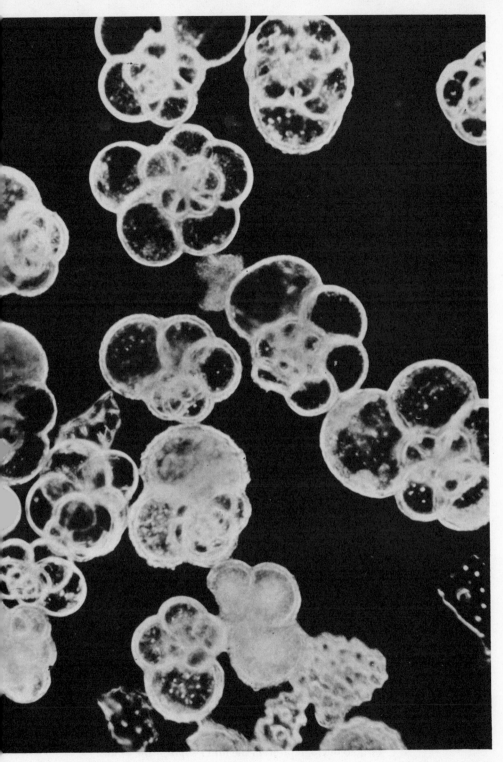

Foraminifera, taken from the sea-floor ooze, more than two miles beneath the surface. They are like minute specks of dust until magnified by the microscope. (Photo-micrograph.)

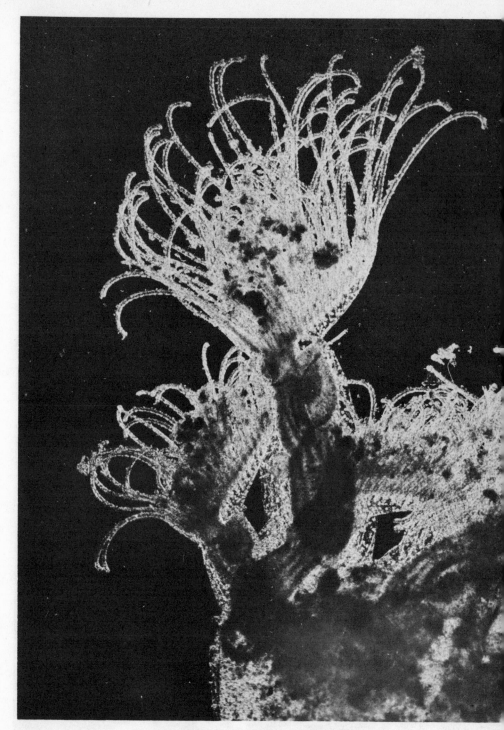

A freshwater polyzoan, a delicate plant-like animal.
(Photo-micrograph from the film *People of the Ponds*.)

friend and Kitty about the ferocity of wild pigs, and the necessity for climbing a tree if they encountered one of these animals.

In the midst of the discussion there was an outburst of grunts and squeals. Some distance away we saw a big boar leading some sows and their families down to the water to drink. It was a night of full moon, and the light was bright enough to shoot by, so I ran back to the camp for my rifle.

One of our party, Pat, a reckless young Irish-Australian, was a keen pig hunter, and without waiting for my return he set his four dogs off on the trail of the pigs. (The next part of the story I heard later.) Pat followed in after the dogs, and an exciting chase commenced in the moonlight. A few hundred yards back from the river the herd of pigs split up and dashed away into the undergrowth with the dogs in pursuit. When Pat caught up with the dogs they were nosing round the undergrowth growing over a huge fallen tree. The dogs started yelping excitedly as a chorus of squeals from young piglets came from a long tunnel in the undergrowth alongside the log. No infuriated mother came out to tackle the dogs, nor was there any sound of grunting. Obviously the mother had left the little pigs while she went to the river for a drink. As there was nothing to fear from young suckers, Pat made his way on hands and knees along the tunnel. Tucking a piglet under each arm he started backing out as there was no room to turn in the narrow tunnel. Then the dogs started barking furiously at a sound of crashing in the undergrowth. This was no place to be found by an infuriated sow returning to her young, so, dropping the piglets, Pat continued backing out as rapidly as possible, only to find that in his hurry he had tangled himself among the creepers.

Desperately, he tried to break free. Amidst the furious barking of the dogs something running swiftly was coming nearer! Pat knew what would happen when the sow arrived. Her one desire would be to reach her young, and she would immediately dash down the tunnel to be brought to a stop by Pat's stern blocking further progress. Her campaign would be opened by a furious rear attack. Pat was not to know that the running feet were mine. I had collected my rifle and cartridges from the camp, and set off at a run towards the sound of barking. When I arrived on the scene, I could hear a furious thrashing amongst the undergrowth, mingled with Pat's yells to the dogs, sooling them on to the attack. Fortunately for me they had accepted me by now as a friendly member of the party, but this did not prevent them from adding to the din with a new outburst of excited barking. It seemed to me that Pat must be having a desperate hand to tusk encounter somewhere under the log, and I shouted encouragement. Hearing my voice he screamed back at me, "Shoot her! Shoot her! Don't let her in here!" This remark sent me running anxiously around the tree to find "her", but my search only showed me the entrance to the tunnel. Down I went on hands and knees and scrambled in the direction of Pat's frenzied yells. After travelling a short distance I was stopped by a barrage of lashing legs. The sow was approaching—as Pat thought— but her victory was not going to be an easy one. A well-placed kick caught me on the top of the head and knocked me flat, whereupon I added my yells to the din. Pat, hearing my yell and the stream of indignant epithets that followed it, quietened down, and now that speed was not necessary, disentangled himself and backed out, but not before he had again secured his piglets. I knew that he was handing one to me when its posterior contacted my face in the darkness. I must say that I prefer meeting my quarry face to face.

After mutual recriminations were over, we returned to camp with our piglets, prepared to receive modestly the admiration which woman-kind so graciously accords the triumphant male, but the womenfolk were not to be found. Our cooees soon brought a faint answer from somewhere along the river bank. We found the ladies—perched high up in a tree! When we had rushed away to the hunt, the ladies had, as instructed, made for the nearest tree and, fearing that the pigs might still be in the vicinity, had remained all this time afraid to leave their perch on a narrow limb of a tree smothered in a prickly creeper. We received but perfunctory thanks for helping them down, and the information that our hunt had been successful was received without enthusiasm; they appeared to be too busy pulling thorns from their persons.

As pigs were plentiful in this locality I unpacked the movie cameras next morning and prepared to make a film of a wild-pig hunt. Pat had a most spectacular accomplishment. He would set the dogs off after a pig, while he followed on foot with a long hunting knife as his only weapon. While the dogs engaged the attention of the pig, he would run in and, catching the pig by its hind legs, throw it off its feet. Then, giving a quick thrust with his knife, he would spring clear. This is a most dangerous method of killing wild pig, which is one of the most savage and courageous of wild animals. I had never seen it attempted before, and considered it would be thrilling motion-picture material.

Pat soon had the dogs on the trail of a pig, while I brought up the rear with the camera. It was not long before we heard excited barking. We followed the sound through the bush and down to the bank of what, in the wet season, was a river, but was now bone dry. The dogs had bailed up a big boar. On sighting us it turned and made off with the dogs in full cry. The boar did not attempt to run up the steep bank and take to the bush, but kept to the dry river bed. About a half-mile farther down I could see where the river bed made a wide sweep and returned on its course only two or three hundred yards from where we stood; so I told Pat that I would run across and set the camera up on the near river bank, while he followed up the pig and helped the dogs to keep the pig moving down the river bed. If the pig could be kept from running up the steep banks it would be certain to pass close to the camera.

I just got the camera set up in time when the pig came racing round the bend towards me. It was great movie material—the pig and dogs in a close bunch with the hunter running only a few feet behind. The dogs were pretty to watch, and showed their careful training. Two of them kept snapping at the pig's heels to keep it moving, while the two best dogs were running neck and neck with the pig, one on each side. It almost seemed as if those dogs signalled to each other. The dog on one side would feint as if it were going to dash at the pig, whereupon the pig would turn its head towards it. Immediately the dog on the other side would leap in. As the formidable tusks swung towards it, that dog would spring clear while the other dog made a quick rush on the other side. This slowed the pace of the boar and gave the hunter a chance to catch up. They were close to the camera by now, and I yelled to Pat to do his stuff. A quick sprint and he had the pig by the hind legs, then came a heave—and over went the pig. When he drove in his knife he unfortunately placed his foot on the pig, and one of the dogs, which had been dashing wildly round looking for a place to take hold, jumped in and fastened his teeth through the toe of Pat's sandshoe and into the pig. There he was—pinned! For a few seconds there was a lovely mix-up; dogs, pig, and man, all down in the dust together. It is just as well that I was not filming in sound, the language would never have passed the censor. Even though the situation was serious it was too good a picture to lose, and instead of going to his assistance, I kept the camera turning. Fortunately the knife-thrust had been a deadly one, and after but a brief struggle the pig was dead. Pat came walking nonchalantly out of the dust cloud as if nothing unusual had happened.

The next day we arrived at the foot of the mountain which the native lugger-boy had described to me. The car had to be deserted here, for the lower slopes of the mountain were covered with a dense tropical jungle. Into this jungle we pushed our way, carrying the coils of rope that might be needed if we were to explore this hole in the mountain.

On our way through that tropical jungle orchids and rope-like lianas had to be chopped out of our way with a jungle knife. Orchids had become a mere matter of geography.

As we climbed the way became more open, the last part of the ascent being almost bare rock with a few stunted trees precariously rooted in the crevices. A few more yards, and the summit was reached. We stood there awe-stricken. A huge, roughly circular pit, about a hundred yards in diameter, dropped straight down into the bowels of the earth. It was quite evidently the crater of an extinct volcano that had ceased to be active hundreds of years ago. I tossed a stone over the brink and counted to eleven before a faint whisper of sound echoed up. The walls of the pit were perpendicular except for one place where a landslide had left a steep slope strewn with jagged boulders. The longer we looked at this forbidding view, the more we began to think that there might be something in the native boy's mountain devil, for certainly the atmosphere of the place was eerie. However, I had come all this way to explore it, and was not going to let the mere sight of the place deter me; so, taking the ropes, we cautiously made our way down the slope of the landslide.

As we progressed the slope became more precipitous, and eventually we could go no farther, for the slope ended in a sheer drop. From this position we could get a much better view of the depths. It was now nearly midday and the sun was shining down into the crater. The bottom of it appeared to be carpeted with a smooth lawn which showed bright grass green where the sun struck it. The sunlight made the place look less fearsome, and quite cheerfully I looped one end of the rope around me and prepared to descend. Only as I slid over the edge did I realize how selfishly self-centred one can become in the search for film material, for I caught a glimpse of Kitty's white strained face as she operated the camera to film the descent into the crater. I grinned at her, but all I got in reply was, "This had better be good. I don't want to make a second take." My companions paid the rope out as I made my way down.

Every here and there I had to call out to be lowered until a place was reached where there were hand and footholds. It was more unpleasant to look up than down, for the slow movement of drifting clouds far above gave a queer illusion. It seemed as if the clouds stood still in the sky, while the cliff was slowly bending forward, and at any moment might reach the point where it overbalanced and toppled forward, carrying me with it into the depths.

Eventually the smooth green floor was only a few feet below me, and I prepared to step on to it. My foot touched it—and went through it! I yelled to my friends above to stop lowering me, and clung to the cliff face. What had appeared to be a smooth lawn was actually a lake of icy cold water with a thin covering of green weed. To my right there was a narrow ledge just a few inches above the water, and I worked my way along until I could crawl on to it. As I looked about me it seemed as if I had invaded this horrible hole in the ground for nothing. All round towered sheer cliffs framing a remote patch of sky like a piece of vivid blue enamel being dusted by the little white clouds. Not even a crevice that might be the entrance to a cave broke the face of the cliff.

There was only one place in which any living creature might exist, and that was in the water. I always carry a small pocket miscroscope with me, and reaching down I scooped up a little water and examined it under the lens. This lake deep in the earth teemed with life! All kinds of microscopic creatures were busily swimming about as happy in a drop of water as a whale in the ocean. A piece of weed from the surface of the lake showed many varieties of microscopic animals adhering to it. I called to my friends above to lower a bottle. The contents of a thermos were soon disposed of, and fastening it to a long fishing line, they lowered the empty flask, which I filled with water and weeds.

Getting down into the crater had been unpleasant enough, but the journey back was a ghastly experience. My feet throbbed with a fiery ache from supporting my weight with mere toeholds on the cliff face, and my hands were slippery with sweat. In many places the cliff face sloped outwards to overhanging ledges, and I could climb no farther, but would have to call to those on top to haul me higher. Up I would go, inch by inch. Every time they paused in their hauling, I would imagine their hands slipping on the rope—and then my quick rush and plunge into the lake beneath me, where, if not killed by striking the water, I would swim hopelessly round like a rat in a bucket, until I grew weak and weary enough to sink quietly beneath the water weeds. Then the slow ascent would begin again, and, slowly spinning round like a spider on the end of a web, I would rub the sweat from my eyes and anxiously watch the rope, which was chafing on the overhanging cliff edge, while I fervently wished I were a few stone lighter. It was a great relief to reach the top; but it had been a worthwhile venture, for the contents of the thermos flask gave enough material for the film *People of the Ponds*.

Hundreds of years ago in this extinct volcano, Nature had carried out an experiment made only yesterday by the famous Pasteur. Until Pasteur's experiment proved otherwise, it was a general belief that life, like Topsy, "just growed". According to this belief neither parents nor seeds were necessary to give rise to swarm of little creatures called animalcules. It was thought that if you put aside a jar, say of soup, and a few days later found that it had gone bad, the little creatures that now swarmed within it had been brought into existence by a process known as spontaneous generation; and it was assumed that the creatures had had no existence whatever until they just suddenly came into being. Pasteur's experiment proved the theory of spontaneous generation to be a fallacy. He took two carefully sterilized test tubes, and placed in each tube a solution which was readily inhabited by microscopic life. Both the test tubes, and the medium within them, were sterilized by heat, and any life that had once been there was thus killed. Pasteur corked one tube with a sterile plug, the other was left uncorked. Within a few days, life flourished in the uncorked tube; but the plugged tube was still sterile, though its contents were just as favourable a medium as that of the uncorked tube wherein millions of animalculae now swarmed. And so Pasteur proved that life did not arise by spontaneous generation; for a simple plug had prevented any life from growing within one of the tubes.

Where then did this life in the uncorked test tube came from? The experiment proved that it could only have come from the air, which had free access to the uncorked tube.

Nature, in her carrying out of this experiment, had fashioned a gigantic test tube from the crater of the volcano, and had sterilized it with the mighty fires from within. For many centuries no life could have existed in the awful heat of the volcano. The molten rock which gushed out in those days must have seared all in the vicinity, and poisonous gases belching forth destroyed all life within reach. Then that huge sterilized test tube in the earth had cooled as the volcanic fires died down. As the centuries passed, distilled water falling from the clouds had made in the crater a lake most suitable as a medium to support water life, and that life had come to it, borne upon the winds.

Nature had not plugged her test tube, for she is a lover of life, and a prolific mother.

CHAPTER 18

PEOPLE OF THE PONDS

W E have already considered the extraordinary variety of microscopic life in the sea, but here in the lake in the crater we find life
of a type not found in the sea. The food medium in the crater has not
been seasoned with salt, and the withholding of those grains of salt
in this fresh water has resulted in a myriad of plants and creatures
different from those that flourish in the salty ocean.

Here again in the fresh water we find the ubiquitous diatoms; but
some species flourish here that were not found when we swept the
sea with the tow-net. However, the fresh water also contains the silica
required to build their lovely skeletons, and other chemical elements
for the development of each little vegetable cell.

Competing with the diatoms in the beauty of their contours and
embellishments are the desmids, another of the single-celled plants.
But the beauty of the desmid is evanescent, for in its short life it
secretes no silica with which to build a lasting skeleton to support the
protoplasm of the minute cell. Some species are only a thousandth of
an inch in diameter, but wonderfully regular and symmetrical in their
design. Beneath the microscope the chlorophyll in their cells gives them
the appearance of strangely cut emeralds, for they have the true
limpid green of those gems. Within them the mechanism of life's
processes can be seen at work, and the circulation of the cell contents
clearly observed. Desmids are peculiar to fresh water and are never
found living in the sea.

Like worlds rolling majestically through space, the *Volvox* swims
into view. Verdant worlds indeed! Like the desmid the *Volvox* is a
vivid green, for its cells also contain chlorophyll. *Volvox* is a perfect
sphere of fine network. Each knot in the mesh is a small green cell
with two minute hairs that vibrate with great rapidity. Since there are
hundreds of little cells in each *Volvox*, with the hairs all lashing the
water in unison, the combined result is to cause the *Volvox* to roll
through the water like a ball rolling along the ground. Where the

sun strikes the surface of the water, they may be found congregated in such numbers that the water appears a bright green. Since each *Volvox* is but one twenty-fifth of an inch in diameter, it can be readily realized what countless thousands are required to cause this coloration. Within the hollow sphere are seen several small circular bodies that, although confined, revolve within the network of the larger sphere. These are the daughter cells, and eventually the wall of the *Volvox* bursts and these small cells roll out through the ruptured walls to carry on a separate existence. When they in turn reach their full development, other daughter cells develop within them.

For many years zoologists accepted the *Volvox* as an animal, and enrolled it as a member of their branch of science. Then the botanists claimed it as a plant, as they had done with many other organisms claimed by the zoologists. Further observations seemed to prove that the botanists were right, and *Volvox* was indeed a vegetable cell. One can almost imagine a zoologist saying to his wife, "My dear, here comes that botanist fellow, Smith. Slip out into the backyard and hide my pet elephant in the wood shed. Nothing's safe from these botanists!"

The zoologists, however, were not satisfied to accept the evidence advanced by the botanists in their claims to the *Volvox*, and so made further researches into the life history of this organism. Now the zoologists have repossessed *Volvox* as a protozoan colony—a colony of primitive animals.

In our observation of the life of the sea we discovered that we could no longer think of worms as rather uninteresting-looking things, and here in the fresh water we also find worms of great interest and beauty. There are an enormous variety of worms; Professor Huxley described them as a "heterogeneous mob".

The microscopic creatures of the fresh water that are almost sure to be the first to catch the eyes are the rotifers. It is believed by some authorities that they have evolved from the worms, being descended from ancestors resembling the larvae of the true worms. The rotifers are highly organized in their structure, and because of the peculiarly hyaline character of their outer surface, all the internal organs can be examined as if seen through a window. *Rotifer vulgaris* has a stream-lined transparent body like a torpedo made of glass, and the similarity goes even farther, for as it swims rapidly into view it would appear that two tiny propellers are revolving at one of its extremities. It is these "propellers" which give it the name rotifer, because of their resemblance to rotating wheels. Actually they are discs borne upon the head of the creature. Round the circumference of these discs are long, fine hairs, called cilia, that lash the water rhythmically. Picture a field of growing wheat: as we watch it a gust of wind blows across it and, as each head of wheat bows in succession, it would seem as if the field of wheat flowed like water. The cilia of the rotifers move in this same flowing fashion. These cilia-bearing discs are used not only to propel the creature through the water, but as a means of securing its food. As the rotifer swims along it will stop abruptly, the end of its body forking into two toe-like projections. With these it will grip some debris or water weed and, while it is thus anchored, the two little discs on its head again commence to whirl, creating a vortex in the water that draws the microscopic life down to the mouth situated at the base of the apparently rotating wheels. When we see them thus we can readily appreciate the elegance of these little creatures. Their integument resembles a transparent tissue of silver through which the internal organs of mastication and digestion are seen as clearly as if housed in glass. It is amazing to think that though such a complicated creature it is so minute that one hundred and twenty-five thousand could be packed into one cubic inch.

The female rotifers are more commonly seen, in fact the male of some species has yet to be discovered. The male is usually much smaller than the female, and in some species his life must be short, for he has no organs for masticating or digesting food. However, he is necessary to fertilize the thick-shelled winter eggs, for a female rotifer produces three kinds of eggs, not only winter eggs as already mentioned, but large and small summer eggs. The male is not required for the development of these summer eggs; they are parthenogenetic, a word meaning produced by a virgin, for these eggs are fertile although the female has never mated. When a male and female mate, the female produces a different kind of egg, which has the ability to withstand the most adverse conditions. It may have to lie in a frozen pool throughout the winter, or, if the water in which it lies is evaporated by the heat of the sun, the winds may lift it with the dust and transport it for many miles. So came our rotifer to the volcano crater in the form of an air-borne egg which, falling into the lake, commenced to develop; and soon the young rotifer broke through its thick shell to do its share in populating the lake in the crater.

Another rotifer named *Brachionus*, instead of having the torpedo shape of *R. vulgaris* is short and broad, like a crystal goblet set upon a flexible stem. This stem is a long, muscular foot ending in forked prehensile toes with which the creature anchors itself in the same manner as do many of the rotifers. It uses these toes as a pivot upon which it swings in dizzying circles. At the mouth of the goblet-shaped body are the "rotating wheels" which whirl the small life in the water into the waiting mouth. *Brachionus* at meal times bears a ridiculous resemblance to the nozzle of a vacuum cleaner being swung wildly in all directions. Against the body, close to the base of the flexible foot, may be seen the eggs throughout all stages of their development. Suddenly the forked toes release their hold and, with discs whirling, *Brachionus* glides away, withdrawing her long telescopic foot into her body as she goes.

But not all rotifers swim freely in the water; some build gelatinous transparent homes from which they protrude heads of exquisite loveliness. My reader may consider that I over-emphasize this beauty. In defence I give you the scientific name of one of these tube-dwelling rotifers—*Floscularia ornata*, so you see that even science has taken note and mentioned what an ornate creature is this tiny speck of life.

Still fresh in my memory is my first sight of a floscule. It was attached to a piece of water weed, and through the walls of its transparent home I could see the creature within. But its beauty was at first not apparent, for the creature was contracted; the handling it had received while the weed was being placed under the microscope had caused the timid creature to shrink deep within the protection of its filmy sheath. As I watched, it slowly relaxed. The head portion, or corona, was like a fragile cup with a scalloped rim, and from the mouth of the cup gleamed what at first sight appeared to be a long blue flame. Actually this was a cluster of long hairs finer than the finest gossamer, and lying in parallel lines so closely together that they formed a refraction screen through which played the scintillating blue light. The cup-like corona expanded more widely, and the blue changed to a delicate green. Then, without warning, the creature spread open like a gorgeous flower blossoming. No longer did the blue or green flame flicker from the centre of the cup, for those long, fine hairs were attached to the scallops on the edge of the rim, and as the cup opened wider and wider the hairs fanned out in the water. So fine were they that it was difficult to see where they ended as they spread out like a halo about the head of the floscule. Within the cup a circle of shorter hairs vibrated rhythmically like the "wheels" of the free-swimming rotifers, and created little whirlpools which carried the food down into the cup. Some small creatures attempted to escape, but those long filaments, which fanned so far out into the water, were a web of death for any small creature caught in the vortex, and would close in to bar its escape. Gradually the number of imprisoned creatures increased, upon which the cup abruptly contracted, making a compact little parcel of the victims, which were then forced down to the jaws that could be seen through the transparent body of the floscule.

Another rotifer that builds a filmy home is *Stephanoceros*, the crown animalcule. Its head is adorned with a large and elaborate crown similar in design to the crown of a royal personage. Although very beautiful, at first sight it would seem rather a useless piece of ornamentation to be worn by such a tiny creature. Smaller microscopic animals swimming in the water surrounding the *Stephanoceros* swim through the openings in the framework of the crown, and can be seen moving about inside. It would seem that these little creatures find conditions within the crown so much to their liking that they have no wish to leave, for never a one of them swims out again. Place a lens of higher power on the microscope and look again. Now we can examine the interior of the crown, and its secret is revealed. This is no useless piece of ornamentation—that crown is a deadly trap. As the creatures attempt to swim out again through the framework, they are driven back by innumerable little whips, rows and rows of vibrating hairs that line the interior of the crown. At the bottom of the crown the hungry mouth of *Stephanoceros* waits for the lashing whips to drive its doomed victims into its open mouth. In both floscule and *Stephanoceros* the young may be seen developing within the sheath-like home of the parent. When the time comes for them to take up life on their own, they bore their way to the outer world through the wall of the parent's home.

The penetrating eye of the microscope can peer even farther into the sex life of the rotifers. I have seen beneath the lens, within the body of another species of rotifer (*Asplanchna*) her as yet unborn daughters, bearing within their bodies *their* unborn daughters. Three generations in one—grandmother, daughters and grandaughters—two of those generations as yet unborn!

Perhaps the quaintest member of the tube-dwelling rotifers is *Melicerta*. More than 250 years ago in the little town of Delft in Holland, a Dutchman, Anton van Leeuwenhoek, saw and described this rotifer. A cranky man was Leeuwenhoek, but a born naturalist. Although the microscopes of those days were but primitive instruments, he discovered and described with amazing accuracy details of the structure of much minute life. A thrifty soul, delighted with the new world opened to him by his first magnifying glass, he wished for better lenses in order that he might see still more. But buy lenses? Not he! So Leeuwenhoek learned the art of grinding lenses for himself, and astonishingly good lenses they were. He was continually grinding more lenses of which he was inordinately proud, even setting them in gold and silver mounts. He would allow people to look at his queer beasties as long as they did not touch one of his microscopes. If they did so he would storm at them with a tirade of abuse and drive them from his house. Although Leeuwenhoek could have sold his miscroscopes for much money, no offer of purchase interested him, nor would he make a gift of his cherished lenses. A difficult man; and yet perhaps his was a viewpoint similar to that of Omar Khayyam when he wrote:

> *I wonder often what the Vintners buy*
> *One half so precious as the goods they sell.*

Although it is so many years since Leeuwenhoek discovered and described *Melicerta*, comparatively few people have watched this strange little rotifer build its brick house. It begins the task by affixing itself to some weed or debris in the water, and then, with its rotating discs, of which it possesses four, it draws in the water, and cements together floating particles of debris, thus manufacturing a tiny brick. Bending forward, it deposits this brick on the support to which it has attached itself. Straightening up, it sets its little "wheels" whirling again, and soon another little brick is placed in position alongside the first; and so the work goes on, a new brick being fashioned every two or three minutes and added to the growing structure. In a very short time it has built a little circular tower from which its head projects with the four little wheels still whirling, looking much like a tiny model of a Dutch windmill. *Melicerta* can be made to build a house of coloured bricks by placing it in a drop of clean water and then adding some finely ground-up colouring matter. All is grist that comes to *Melicerta's* mill, and it sets to work extracting the colouring matter from the water. If the material added is red, then little red bricks will be made. When all the red is exhausted from the water and some powdered chalk is added, a ring of white bricks will be deposited above the red. Now as the mill of *Melicerta* pauses for fresh material, add blue colouring to the water, and soon the head of *Melicerta* will project from the top of a dainty little red, white, and blue home.

In the lifetime of the world it is but yesterday since man was a cave dweller, and it is not at all unlikely that an ancestor of yours, or mine, bending down to drink like an animal from stream or pool, was only a few inches away from *Melicerta*, the expert little builder. But it was to be many centuries before man would be capable of making his home of bricks.

In the crater lake, crustaceans were represented by the Entomostraca, which means an animal within a shell. Although the Entomostraca belong to the same class (Crustacea) as the freshwater crayfish, the lobsters, and crabs, one would hardly think so from the very different appearance of these tiny animals. When first discovered they so resembled that pest called *Pulex irritans*, the flea, that they received the name *Daphnia pulex*, or water fleas. Early observers thought that the pointed beaks were used to plunge into the victims and suck up their blood. But *Daphnia* has no penchant for human blood, nor is its sharp, pointed beak used to obtain food; its five pairs of feet are used for this purpose. Its outer case is hinged along the back, and opens along the front as does the shell of the oyster. Through this opening *Daphnia* secures both food and oxygen. Inside the transparent valves of the shell the legs may be seen working like tiny paddle-wheels drawing in the water from which the creature extracts oxygen for respiration. At the same time it sieves out any nutritious substance for food, and moulds it with its feet into a conveniently sized pellet to be transferred to the mandibles for mastication. The progress of the food along the digestive canal can be clearly traced as the peristaltic action (or worm-like contractions of the canal) drives the food through the body of the creature. The pulsating heart, and just beneath it the developing eggs in the body of the mother, are also plainly displayed. When the young are sufficiently developed, they seize the opportunity, when the shells of the mother are apart, to escape into the surrounding water. *Daphnia's* feet being in almost constant motion, it really appears as if she kicks her children out of the house. Since she uses her feet to kick her food into her mouth, *Daphnia* swims by using the long, branched antennae as paddles. At each brisk stroke of the antennae, she moves through the water in a series of abrupt, jerky jumps, another characteristic that reminded early observers of the flea.

Water fleas have two types of eggs, the winter and summer eggs, and from only one type of eggs are males at certain periods produced. The adult male is much smaller than the female, and not nearly so elaborate in structure. However, they are quite capable of fertilizing the second type of egg. This egg has a thick and tough shell, which can survive extreme variations in temperature, and is not destroyed by dessication. If the water dries up during a long dry summer, the egg remains unharmed in the dust, and may be lifted by the winds and transported over great distances. The dust from dry areas of Australia has been frequently carried across the Tasman Sea to be deposited in New Zealand more than a thousand miles away. It was by this method of aerial transport that the first water flea was able to reach the lake in the crater of the volcano.

You may wonder, if only one egg reached the water in the crater, how it could possibly result in the development of countless generations of water fleas. The explanation is very wonderful. From a thick-shelled, fertilized egg carried into the crater by the wind, a female water flea is born. One would expect this lone lorn female to live her life out as a spinster, and perish. But this is not so. Within a remarkably short period, eggs commence developing within her brood chamber. Soon they are active young water fleas moving about within the body of the mother, and before long they leave the shelter of the brood chamber to take up life on their own account. These young *Daphnia* are also females, and soon eggs develop within them, and they in turn give birth to swarms of new female water fleas, which continue producing more female babies. There is not one male water flea in the community of the crater, and yet the females are capable of producing offspring. As the warm days of summer continue, the crater lake swarms with countless thousands of female water fleas all busy producing more female babies. But as the autumn winds whisper of the colder days ahead, and the food supplies commence to dwindle, a momentous event takes place: the water fleas now commence to produce male babies which fertilize the eggs of the females. These eggs grow large and thick shelled, and do not hatch out rapidly as the eggs have done throughout the summer and early autumn. Soon the lake has lost its busy water fleas, and any dead *Daphnia* that are found may still have these last eggs lying within them. Although the bodies of the water fleas are disintegrating, the fertilized winter eggs are secure in their thick, tough shells, and remain quiescent through the chill days of winter. The warm days of spring awake the sleeping power within the eggs, and incubation begins. Soon from all the hundreds of thousands of eggs in the crater lake, the new generation of female water fleas bursts forth; no males, just thousands of females whose eggs develop with the extraordinary fecundity of these amazing spinsters. As spring glides into summer, and summer into autumn, the lake teems with millions of unmated females, busily bringing forth generation after generation of water fleas.

The thermos flask of water and weeds held our party captive for some days. I had unpacked the spare microscope and left it to my companions to amuse themselves with while I worked at the filming of *People of the Ponds*. No one wanted to explore the surrounding jungle: the members of the party spent most of the day peering into the microscope, with the result that each night round the camp-fire, the questions and answers about life and its purpose and origin were as plentiful as the bats which flitted about our camp.

Whilst the microscope had given Paula, our journalist friend, her first glimpse of these queer microscopic animals, their existence was not unknown to her; but poor Pat was bewildered. He was a first-class bushman, a keen observer, and a natural naturalist; but he had never imagined that there was an invisible world on earth peopled by such weird and incomprehensible inhabitants. His simple soul and mind

A fairy fly, so tiny that with wings outspread it could pass through
the eye of a needle. (Photo-micrograph.)

The eggs of a moth. The fairy fly pierces insect eggs like these
and lays her eggs inside them. (Photo-micrograph.)

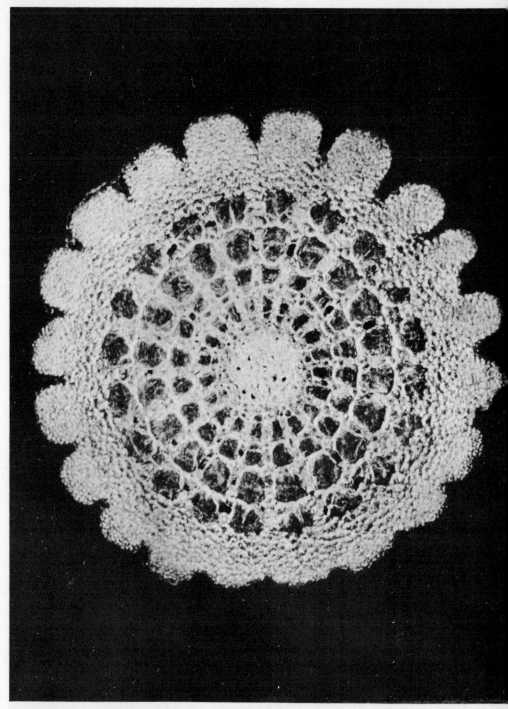

A thin slice from the spine of a sea urchin. (Highly magnified; photo-micrograph from the film *Secrets of the Sea*.)

were in revolt against the new and disturbing thoughts that the sight of each new creature evoked. Paula, rather cruelly I thought, delighted in increasing his bewilderment by remarks contrary to the orthodox theological beliefs Pat had accepted from childhood. The arguments came to a climax when Paula maliciously told Pat that an ameoba, a shapeless piece of slime they were watching beneath the microscope, looked exactly like Pat's first ancestor. Pat could stand no more, and heatedly quoted voluminous extracts from the Bible.

The answer of science to this vexed question is taken from fossilized evidence writ as deep and clear in stone as were the Ten Commandments. Millions of years went into the creation; each step along the tangled pathway of evolution was slow; and each false step was obliterated. There is nothing in the law of evolution that would deny the Deity: evolution makes only more majestic the Creator of such a law.

Pasteur's experiment supplied us with the explanation of how life had become so abundant in the volcano lake. It would seem reasonable to assume that, when our infant earth cooled and was no longer a flaming mass of molten elements, the cosmic dust from outer space raining down on the world sowed the seeds of earth's first life. Of course, this first life would have had to survive the awful cold of the void. A French scientist, Paul Becquerel, has shown that life can survive under such conditions. Becquerel put dried bacteria and spores for weeks into the intense cold of liquid air. (A block of ice in comparison to the temperature of liquid air would have the heat of molten metal.) Yet, after such drastic treatment, the spores and bacteria became active again, and were soon busy with the function of reproduction.

But how did those early forms of life, as they travelled on through space, escape the lethal bombardment of ceaseless cosmic rays? Any organisms must surely have reached our earth as frozen corpses, shot through and through by a devastating barrage of invisible projectiles. Pasteur's experiment proves how life could have developed in the crater, but it does not prove how life began on earth. Indeed it is quite possible that life *did* originate by a process of spontaneous generation!

There is scientific evidence that from organisms like some still living in the volcano not only the plants but also the animal kingdom arose. These primitive organisms are called flagellates: minute specks of protoplasm swimming along by the aid of tiny whip-like organs that lash the surrounding water. So primitive are the flagellates that they seem to be neither plants nor animals: some characteristics entitle them to be classified as plants, but other peculiarities would justify them being placed with the animals. The flagellates were not the first living organisms on earth: they have evolved from an even more primitive type.

Perhaps the most plausible hypothesis, in the attempt to explain the origin of life, has come from the peculiar behaviour of the viruses. Although so extremely minute that they are invisible beneath the highest powers of the optical microscope, the viruses can be seen in the mass in a crystalline form. No ordinary living substance can survive repeated crystallization; but the viruses do, and when returned to favourable conditions they resume their way of life and begin to multiply. Recent scientific experiments indicate that in the far distant days of the infancy of our world, it is quite possible that some warm primeval pool contained in solution all the elements necessary for the existence of a virus-like organism, and that here there developed a protein crystal that eventually evolved into a virus. The evolutionary step from the viruses to the visible bacteria-like organisms may some day be proved, and from the bacteria to the flagellates is a much smaller evolutionary gap to bridge: and so the ladder of evolution leads upwards.

This theory regarding the origin of life leaves us with the fascinating thought that perhaps there is no fundamental difference between organic (living) and inorganic (non-living) matter. They may really be one, but in different forms.

I give thanks to W. H. Carruth the American poet who has summarized this so aptly:

> *A fire-mist and a planet,*
> *A crystal and a cell,*
> *A jellyfish and a saurian,*
> *And cave where the cavemen dwell;*
> *Then a sense of law and beauty,*
> *And a face turned from the clod—*
> *Some call it Evolution,*
> *And others call it God.*

CHAPTER 19

ROBINSON CRUSOE HAD NOTHING ON US

LEAPING LENA rattled and boiled her way back to the coast, pulling up every few miles to have her tires refilled with grass and retied when the ropes became frayed and cut by the stony ground. A gallant old soul was Lena; when she pulled up at the wharf her whole body was still trembling with an eager desire to be off and away again.

Bidding farewell to Paula and Pat, we set sail for our new island on a sea so still and clear that it seemed but the ghost of a sea. There was no horizon; sea and sky merged, and the boat sailed on through a blue nothingness. Our first sight of the island was like the picture of a tiny coral island either hanging on an invisible nail, or painted on the sky. The startled fish in the lagoon darted for the shelter of the coral as our anchor splintered the glassy surface.

Our tent was soon pitched, and the food-supplies, optical bench, microscopes, and cameras, were stored in an old galvanized-iron shed that stood like a monument amidst the debris and rusting machinery of a long-deserted turtle canning factory. The shed had been kept in some sort of repair by visiting fishermen who sometimes ran to the island for shelter in bad weather. This tiny coral island had no natural fresh water-supply, but there was no shortage, as the roof of the shed drained into a big tank that, long ago, had supplied the old turtle canning factory.

The crew waved us cheery good-byes as the boat slid through the break in the reef on its journey back to the mainland. It was to return in two weeks with fresh stores, and would take back our film for dispatch to the south. For a fortnight we would be the king and queen of a peaceful coral kingdom, our only subjects the hordes of sand crabs, sea birds, geckos, spiders, cockroaches, and visiting turtles. We looked forward very happily to those two weeks of uninterrupted peace —peace that would give us an opportunity to explore a new reef, and to push ahead with the microscopic film, *Secrets of the Sea*. But there was one secret that we did not know: it was to be six weeks before our supply boat would once more drop anchor in the lagoon.

Right on the trailing skirts of the sudden tropic sunset came the first visit of one section of our island subjects. There was a sound like hail on the top of our tent, and then along the ridge pole flowed a shining brown stream of cockroaches; large, winged beasts with the dazzling speed of Arab steeds. We rolled up newspapers and with lusty bangings tried to bring our unruly and unwelcome subjects under control. Although we inflicted heavy casualties, we had this unpleasant visitation every evening while the calm before the monsoons lasted. The numbers of the loathsome brutes never seemed to dwindle, although each night we swept the fallen up in heaps and fed them to the fish in the lagoon.

After a few nights we were joined by formidable allies, triantelopes; huge hairy spiders almost six inches across, which, outspeeding the fleetest cockroach, sprang like tigers on to their prey, and drove deep into the victim's bodies a pair of long curved fangs. The only fault we had to find with the triantelopes was their incurable habit of sitting down to a banquet while the battle still raged. Not until an uneasy peace was restored did those quaint little lizards, the geckos, come "geec-koing" along. They were no warriors, merely the internal stretcher bearers of the dead and wounded.

If "man bites dog" is news, then surely "spider bites lizard" is equally worthy of headlines. One of the timbers in the roof of the store shed was pierced by a bolt hole, and a lady gecko, obviously in an interesting condition, was in search of a place to deposit her burden of eggs. Spying the bolt hole, she waddled forward to inspect its possibilities as a nursery. As she put her head into the hole, the head of another gecko slid cautiously into view on the top of the beam, and the little bright eyes peered down at the lady with the eggs. The prospective mother crawled into the hole, leaving only her long tail waving about outside. Like a flash, the gecko on top of the beam darted down, gave the waving tail a sharp nip, and fled back out of sight behind the beam. The investigating gecko awkwardly backed her bulky body out of the hole and glared round while she indignantly muttered a string of "geec-kos" like a tiny time-bomb. Since nothing was in sight, she eventually commenced to explore the hole again. As soon as only her waving tail projected, down flashed her tormentor, and again she received a snappy bite on the tail. This happened several times, and I felt obliged to put the whole thing down to a malicious sense of humour, and to accept the fact that geckos are born practical jokers.

While I was pondering this matter, tragedy made a startling entry. The mischievous gecko had just given a nip and scampered back to its place of concealment when there was a flashing blur of a hurtling hairy body, and the poor practical joker was struggling in the grasp of a huge triantelope. The long fangs that had been plunged into the gecko's abdomen were suddenly withdrawn, and as the spider straddled the gecko it sank those needle-sharp poison fangs firmly into its neck. A few spasmodic wriggles and the gecko was limp, while the triantelope, with its row of beady eyes gleaming, crouched down over the body to enjoy the feast. Spider not only bit, but ate, lizard.

Our cameras had been so busy that it seemed no time before the boat was almost due again. We woke the morning before it was expected to an almost suffocatingly oppressive heat. The air felt stagnantly still; it was an effort to do any work. The least exertion started the sweat pouring out of the skin, and our eyes were smarting from a perpetual eyebath of perspiration. Still, there was always the cool lagoon to make things bearable.

For the first time the usually crystal-clear water was a disappointment. It was like warm soup full of myriads of planktonic animals. Long chains of salps, looking like tiny glass barrels strung together, weaved their way like miniature railway trains through masses of a reddish scum which proved to be countless billions of microscopic algae. Here and there, through a break in the surface scum, we caught flashes of coloured lights like pieces of rainbow moving through the still water. The lagoon was full of sea gooseberries. Each of these animals was about half an inch in length and at first glance bore a resemblance to a transparent gooseberry. Eight crescent-shaped bands with comb-like plates in vertical rows adorn their crystal clear bodies. From these plates emanate the tiny rainbows. Each plate is lined with a delicate fringe of minute hairs that, all waving in unison, propel the creature along. As the sunlight catches the waving hairs, the light is diffracted into flashes of gleaming iridescence. These lovely little animals are accomplished fishermen, keeping their fishing lines neatly packed away in two sac-like cavities in the body. As we watched, the lines were extended several times the length of the creature's body and some tiny creatures were snared, whereupon the lines were quickly hauled in with the luckless captives still futilely struggling to break free.

There could be no pleasure in swimming in the already crowded lagoon; so, taking the tow-nets, we started up the engine in our small boat and, slicing a track through the red scum, sailed out from the lagoon into the open sea. After several attempts to use the tow-nets we gave up in disgust. So prolific was the plankton that the nets hardly had time to sink beneath the surface before they were completely clogged and would have to be lifted up again, filled with a quivering gelatinous mass of sea animals so tightly packed together that they could not be separated and sorted into species. Still, it was more pleasant in the boat than on the island, for the forward movement gave us the semblance of a breeze, and we lay back and gazed up at the clear blue sky while the boat chugged smoothly along.

A sudden lurch of the boat and a splash of cold sea water brought me out of a doze. There was no wind, but the sea was no longer glassy calm. We were two or three miles away from the island, and I swung the boat round and started the run back. Then I saw a white line across the sea rushing towards the boat, and the sea whitened round us as a short blast of wind struck us. It passed on, and the air was once more still and oppressive. Telling Kitty to take over the tiller and make straight back for the island, I scrambled forward to the engine and pushed the throttle wide open. The short gusts became more frequent and were now hitting the boat in vicious jabs. No longer was the sky a clear blue; the fierce buffeting of the rising wind was leaving big patches like purple black bruises, and speeding across the ugly sky were hundreds of sea birds making for the island.

It was really a nasty sea now—not waves, but a higgeldy-piggeldy mass of sharp peaks, and sudden hollows, and the jerky lurches and bumps were bringing too much water aboard. I thought it wiser to keep the engine at full speed than to ease our way through the rising seas; so, taking the kicking tiller from Kitty, who immediately started bailing, I turned more closely into the wind and made for the nearest point of the island. Although there was no break in the reef near the point, we would be in the lee of the island and in less danger of swamping. The seas were boiling and surging on the reef as we skirted along the edge towards the break into the lagoon. The sky looked unnatural and terrifying. It was now a dark purplish colour, with one ominous patch of a bright, bronzy-green. We shot through the entrance into the lagoon, which, reflecting the queer greenish light in the sky, looked like a huge beaten copper tray pressed against the side of the island. Picking up the moorings, we made the boat secure and waded towards the shore. That usually immaculate white strip of coral sand had a very piebald appearance now, for right along the beach were big groups of huddled sea birds. The dark patches they made on the beach were ever expanding as an endless stream of birds raced in to flop hurriedly down among their fellows.

Tropical storms are sudden but usually soon over, and after hammering the tent pegs more firmly into the ground I slackened off the tent ropes in case we might get a shower of rain. With everything put shipshape about the camp, we sat down to cool off, for it was still oppressively hot.

It was a weird scene. That purple-black sky, with the bronze slit pouring down an unearthly greenish light, and above us a group of frigate birds wheeling with motionless wings, like vampire bats on the cover of a horror magazine. The wind was rapidly growing into a real gale, and far off we heard a distant roar like rolling thunder. Good! Rain would cool the air down and make things a lot more comfortable. But surely a peal of thunder would not have lasted so long, and sound as if it were racing towards us.

The frigate birds swooped earthwards and the cyclone struck!

Compared to this the previous wind had been only a breeze. It yammered, shrieked, and moaned with the deep sound of a growling beast. The tops of the taller trees had no time to bow, they just snapped straight off and hurtled along above the island jungle.

We were dazed not only by the fury of the storm, but by the noise that accompanied it. My ears felt as if I was down in the diving suit with the pressure of the sea pushing them inwards. Kitty tugged at my arm; I could see her lips move, but could hear only the frenzied shriek of the cyclone. She pointed to where our tent had been pitched. It was gone. Our broken camp beds were jammed up against the trees about two hundred yards away, but the tent—we never saw a sign of it again. Kitty clung to me to prevent herself being blown away as we fought our way to the old galvanized-iron shed. Here the shelter of the jungle broke some of the raging force of the wind, but now the rain came. It was like an insane nightmare. The sky was a never-ending blaze of lightning, the torrential rain could have been falling silently for all we could hear through the noise of that fury of rushing air. Water began to find its way through all the chinks in the old shed. Microscopes, motion-picture cameras, and gear of that sort are not improved by water, and I searched round the shed for a dry place. It was hopeless; the shed was running water like a shower bath! Then I thought of a big iron vat bolted down to the concrete floor of the ruined turtle factory. Rusted it certainly was, but no rain could penetrate it, and not even this mad wind could tear it free from that concrete floor. Although the distance was short, every trip to the vat was a battle with the wind and rain, but in there it was dry. The mast and sails of our little boat were in the shed and I took the sails across to the vat to make a place for Kitty to lie on. The sails would not be needed on the boat again: when struggling back to the shed I had seen the shattered remnants of the boat amongst the trees fringing the beach. It had been torn from its moorings and swept ashore in the enormous waves that were smashing far back amongst the trees.

The last trip to the vat, with the few provisions left in the shed, was the most difficult of all. All the trees at one point had been blown flat, and the wind raged across the island without hindrance. The roof had lifted off the shed while I was gathering the last of the food, and I was only about half-way to the vat when sheets of galvanized iron on the shed walls started to rip free and race away before the wind as if they were sheets of newspaper. Kitty took the food from me and insisted that I crawl into the vat. I was just looking for a place in our cramped quarters where I could stretch out straight when, with, a reverberating clang, the last tin wall of the old shed wrapped itself round the side of the vat. There was no sign of the cyclone diminishing in fury; if anything, it kept increasing; so we sorted the gear out and got things arranged as comfortably as possible in our iron fortress.

Well, even if we had to stay here for quite sometime we would not be lonely: the vat had a remarkably large population of cockroaches and triantelopes. We watched them by candlelight, as they continued the old game of hunter and hunted, until we fell asleep. When I woke again it was night and the wind had stopped.

It was good to get out of the vat and move round freely. Kitty started up the primus stove, while I took an electric torch and set off to explore the remains of our camp. Our tent was gone, but I rescued our broken beds. They could be repaired. The sodden camp mattresses would soon dry when the sun shone again. Most of our clothes had vanished, but we did not need many. We, the microscopes, the cameras, and our film, were all safe. It could have been much worse. Certainly we did not have much food left, but the boat would be in as soon as the weather settled. When I finished my exploration, Kitty had supper cooked, and steaming fragrant coffee waiting. Why worry about a little thing like a cyclone!

It was just grey dawn when we heard the sinister roaring sound again. We must have been right in the centre of the cyclone. As we clambered back into our refuge, the wind was hammering the island from the opposite direction, and waves were breaking over the place, back from the beach, where our tent had been pitched. If there had been no shelter, I am sure that no one could have lived through the cyclone, for the sand was being driven before the wind and tore at the skin like wet sandpaper. Unless heavily clothed, a man would have been flayed alive in a very short time.

Safely ensconced in our vat, we forgot the cyclone in watching the wooing of a big triantelope female by a more slender, but eager, male. When he first attempted to make advances to the husky Amazon she appeared to regard him more in the light of a prospective dinner than as a prospective lover. Whenever he approached her, she would make a short furious dash towards him; it was plain that her intentions were not amorous, and the male would dart away on a swift zig-zag course. But he was persistent, and each time returned towards her as she halted. Eventually, she let him approach until he was only a short distance from her. Then he commenced to show her his ability as an eccentric dancer. On tiptoe, he moved as gracefully as an eight-legged Nijinsky. She let her body sink down and lay quiet in the centre of her great hairy limbs. The lady was interested. Slowly she turned to face him as he lightly circled round her. The pace grew faster—

what a fine nimble fellow! But what has happened? Has he in the wild ecstasy of his love-dance broken his legs? The four legs on one side of his body have collapsed, and slowly the dancer falls over on to his apparently injured side. But no, he has only tripped, and away he goes again as lightly as a sunbeam on dancing water. Round and round in dizzying circles. Again his legs collapse, this time on the opposite side. Slowly he draws himself up until he stands stiff and dignified before her, then first one set of legs collapse, and then the other, until he see-saws swiftly from side to side, his feet remaining firmly planted. Those long legs seem to be made of pliant indiarubber. Then a new display of virtuosity is added to the repertoire. The palpi at each side of his fangs begin to vibrate, and he semaphores in swiftly moving symbols his burning love for the lady he entertains.

At last, believing in the greatness of his love, she limply relaxes as he exultantly leaps forward to clasp her yielding form in his eight hairy legs. . . .

Gradually the rain ceased and the wind died down to only gale force. Our worries were over, and the air was much cooler. Taking the canvas sail and the axe, I commenced cutting new tent poles over which we draped the sails to make quite a comfortable tent. Even if it was rather open at each end, we had no next-door neighbours to consider.

I was just completing the tent when Kitty came hurrying over with a very worried expression.

"We haven't got any water."

I grinned at her. "Oh no! After all that rain?"

Kitty shook her head doubtfully. "Well, no water runs out of the tap on the tank."

I dropped the axe I had been using to drive in tent pegs and hurried over to the tank.

"I suppose some leaves have blown in, and the tap is blocked," I said. Kitty tapped the tank; it rang hollow.

"Sounds empty," she said.

"Good Lord, it can't be!" Climbing up on top I looked inside. It was. A falling tree had struck the tank a glancing blow, and the old tank had failed to stand up to it. Looking down I could see the light shining in through a burst seam at the bottom. The only drinking water on the island had flowed away through that burst seam into the sand. There was no chance of finding any rain pools on the island. The sandy soil on these small coral islands is like a sieve.

It was still blowing hard, and the supply boat would not leave the mainland until the weather improved. In this hot climate, we had to get drinking water—and get it quickly. I climbed down from the tank, picked up the kerosene-tin we used for holding drinking-water, and started off to the lagoon.

"What are you going to do?" asked Kitty.

"We're going to distil sea water," I answered. "You'll have to officiate as chief brewer with a temporary still until I have built a permanent one."

The kerosene-tin of sea water was soon boiling briskly over a wood fire, and Kitty, wringing a towel out in sea water, spread it over the top of the steaming tin. The rising steam condensed on the cold towel, and, after wringing the towel out and replacing it over the tin a few times to remove the salt from the towel, Kitty set happily to work wringing the towel into her kettle. We would not die of thirst, but something more efficient had to be devised. I remembered seeing pieces of water pipe showing above the ground here and there near the old factory. In its operating days, most likely, water had been piped from the tank to various outhouses. Investigation showed this was so, and I soon had a few long lengths of galvanized pipe dug out. Making the pipe into the coiled spiral that was to act as a condenser worm was not a difficult problem. I poured sand into the pipe to prevent the metal splitting then, with one end of the pipe firmly nailed to the stump of a tree, I walked slowly round the tree pushing the pipe ahead of me until it was wound around the stump in a spiral. When the nails holding the end of the pipe were withdrawn I lifted a really neat job off the stump. A forty-four gallon kerosene-drum with one end of the pipe soldered in the top was filled with sea water. When a fire was built under this drum we would have a large retort. With a cold chisel I cut the top out of another drum and, lowering the spiral pipe into it, punched a hole in the side of the drum near the bottom through which the lower end of the pipe could project: this end of the pipe was soon soldered firmly in place, and this drum was filled with sea water. A good fire was built under the first drum, and I awaited results. The water in the drum over the fire should send steam along the pipe and down the spiral resting in the drum of cold sea water. Here the steam as it travelled through the cold spiral should condense, and emerge from the end of the projecting pipe as fresh water. Since the salt in the water cannot turn to steam it must remain in the drum over the fire.

I heard the water in the drum start boiling, but no water appeared from the pipe projecting from the side of the other drum. Now, unless the steam pressure that must be mounting dangerously in the retort drum could find an outlet, I had a potential bomb! Hurriedly I began to rake out the fire. There was a sudden loud pop and with a devastating hiss steam shot out the end of the pipe. Startled I jumped back, but everything was proceeding according to plan. Evidently, I had not shaken all the sand out of the spiral pipe before installing it in the drum, and this residue had acted as a cork until the mounting pressure blew out the obstruction like a pea from a pea-shooter.

Soon the hissing of steam ceased, and then water started to trickle from the pipe. It was red with rust, but, after all, iron is used in tonics and although not in any need of a tonic, a spot of rust could do me no harm, and I wanted to taste that water. It tasted of rusty pipe, but it was fresh. Gradually the rusty colour disappeared, and a steady trickle of clear water issued from the pipe. With a slow fire burning throughout the day, it was surprising how steadily the water level rose in a bucket placed under the end of the pipe. We had the ocean from which to draw our water-supply, and the cyclone had considerably increased our supply of firewood.

Now we had time to look at the damage done to the island. It seemed impossible that so much could have been changed in so little time. The island jungle had had the appearance of an impenetrable green wall. Now, the trees had been completely stripped of leaves and one could see right across the island. Here and there lanes were cut through where the fallen trees lay in rows; and mixed up with the smashed trees were the torn and twisted bodies of birds. Dead sea birds lay scattered around, and living birds were huddled about on the ground completely exhausted and dazed. Most of them made no attempt to move away, but could be picked up, and would remain abjectly huddled in our hands. Put back on the ground they just squatted down where they were placed. Dead sea birds littered the beach and tossed about in the angry waters of the lagoon. This place, which such a short time ago had been a lovely picture of coral island tranquillity, was now an ugly shambles.

But the change on the sea front was beyond belief. Where our tent had originally been pitched was now part of the lagoon. All the sand had been scoured out and deposited down at the next point, where our favourite coral reef had been. Now, instead of the reef, there was a big dry sand-spit; the coral reef was buried beneath hundreds of tons of sand. All those years, maybe many thousands, of slow building by the coral polyps had been destroyed and hidden in a few short hours. There was no pleasure in further exploration. The pounding seas still spouted high along the outer edge of the reef, and the wind-driven sand on the beach drove us back to the comparative calm amidst the stark trees.

Work was what we needed, and there was plenty to do if we were to have a reasonably comfortable camp again. The next few days showed an orderly camp: our tent of sails was comfortable, our camp beds were mended, and the mattresses dry. Our water-supply plant was very efficient and required only an occasional filling with sea water and building up of the fire. A small shed for a laboratory and store-room was built from pieces of timber and sheets of galvanized iron retrieved from where they had been tossed by the cyclone. Our film work was proceeding satisfactorily.

The weather was still very rough, and we had not yet realized how much the loss of the little boat would hamper us. Food was our biggest problem. There were only a few pounds of flour, and a little sugar; no dried milk or vegetables, no meat, no butter; only three tins of baked beans, a few tins of fruit and jam. Most of our flour had got wet during the cyclone, and soon turned into a green, mouldy mess. As yet, there was no sign of the supply boat, and I was most reluctantly suffering a strict system of tobacco rationing.

When planning our stores we had relied upon a plentiful supply of fish. Under normal conditions, this would have been a certainty, for fish is very plentiful round the coral islands. Kitty had spent a whole day untangling the fishing lines, which we had dug out from the locker on our wrecked boat; but apart from the hooks already on the lines there was no trace of the tin of spare hooks. We sifted the sand most carefully, but the tin must have been washed away. The fish are always plentiful along the edge of coral reefs, but coral seems to have an insatiable appetite for fish hooks, and for nearly every fish caught we sooner or later lost one of our few hooks. Now we had none. Normally, at low tide, fish can be speared in the lagoon, but rough seas made it impossible to see the fish. However, by probing about blindly beneath the coral, occasionally a fish in hiding underneath would give a wriggle, and the spear could be driven home. In good weather, this is one of the surest and quickest methods of securing a meal of fish. One can see the fish as they dart for cover through the shallow water, and see just where they have disappeared into the coral. Then in goes the spear, and—nearly always—out comes a fish, wriggling on the barb. I was spearing a few fish, but not enough to allow us really to fill up on fish and so eke out our tinned supplies. Still, good weather would solve the problem. We would not starve, although our diet might be somewhat monotonous.

I was developing some test film-strips when Kitty called to me that she had sighted a sail. By the time I could finish the job and get down to the beach, the boat was beating up through rough seas to the lagoon entrance. It was the supply boat, and all our worries were over. In fact it seemed as if there had never been anything to worry about.

Down came the sails and, with the engine only, the boat crept cautiously towards the entrance where the seas were surging in a tumbled mass. Suddenly the boat stopped, and we saw the crew running towards the bows and peering down into the sea. We heard faint shouts, and saw much activity along the deck. Then, with the crew waving to us and shouting out some message that the wind tore to pieces, the boat slowly reversed out of the entrance and, to our dismay, swung about. The sails began to rise again as she sailed away towards the mainland. Certainly it was very rough in the channel, but there should be plenty of water under the boat at this stage of the tide. In silence we watched the boat dwindle, then Kitty turned to me with a rueful smile.

"Well, there goes the new lipstick I ordered."

Soon the dead calms were with us again, and the island was beginning to recover from its beating. No longer could one see far through the forest. The trees had spread a dainty curtain of light-green, baby leaves. The birds were rebuilding their nests, and there was a continuous stream of sea birds either going out over the sea to fish, or returning to the island. Green creepers were shrouding heaps of fallen trees, and the litter of debris had gone from the beach. The tides had restored it to its former dazzling whiteness.

With the coming of the calm weather I discovered why the supply boat had not come into the lagoon. The cyclone had torn a huge mass of coral from the edge of the reef, and dumped it down into the channel. There was enough space to sail between the edge of the reef and the mass of jagged coral, but it would have been quite impossible to have picked out a course in the turmoil of tumbled water when the boat had last attempted to enter. Each low tide I worked at clearing away as much of the coral as I could break up with a crowbar, but the main mass would need dynamite to shift it. I cut a stout pole, and nailed a strip of canvas to its top, then jammed it down into the coral with the canvas fluttering about three feet above the reach of the highest tide. When the boat arrived again, the captain would guess what that little flag indicated.

The small boat we had used for dragging the silk tow-nets for collecting microscopic life was now sorely missed, but by floating the nets out on the currents from the edge of the reef at low tide we captured much interesting material to keep the microscope and camera busy. We were not yet too tired of oysters, sea urchins, turtle steaks, and all the fish we could eat; but a cup of tea or coffee would have been wonderful. Bread and butter were the things to dream of.

One morning we were returning to our camp from the far side of the island, where we had been collecting turtle eggs for breakfast, when we saw the supply boat sailing along the edge of the reef on its way to the entrance. We dropped our breakfast and hurried round the beach, arriving at the camp just as the skipper was coming ashore in a dinghy.

We waded out to meet him. He waved, and lifted a bottle of beer from a case alongside him on the seat.

"They make this sort of stuff in Australia now," he called to us. "Thought you might like to sample it."

I smiled appreciatively at the bottle as I swung a box of supplies up on to my shoulder.

"Saw your mark in the channel as we came in," he said, as we walked up the beach to the camp.

"We touched that when we came in before. I couldn't see how much more there was, and didn't know how much damage we had already done. There was no place to beach her here if we couldn't get into the lagoon, so we made back for the mainland. We only stripped some copper. Came back as soon as we had her fixed up. Had no doubts about you two being able to live off the land, and there's tons of water in the tank over there."

The skipper halted and goggled at our still, simmering quietly over its wood fire.

"Say, what's that weird-looking contraption?"

"That's our tons of water," said Kitty, grinning at him impishly.